FRANK BRUNO

From Zero to Hero

FRANK BRUNO
From Zero to Hero

His own knockout story

with Norman Giller

ANDRE DEUTSCH

First published in Great Britain in 1996 by André Deutsch Ltd
106 Great Russell Street, London WC1B 3LJ

Copyright © Hamlet Advertising Ltd. & Norman Giller 1996

British Library Cataloguing in Publication Data
A catalogue record for this book is available
from the British Library

ISBN 0 233 99007 0

Printed and bound in Great Britain by WBC, Bridgend.

*For Laura, Nicola, Rachel
and Franklin Junior.
Thank you for giving
me something
worth fighting for.*

Contents

Authors' Note

The authors wish to acknowledge the important part played by VCI chief executive Steve Ayres in getting this book off the launching pad. Thanks also to Tom Rosenthal and his editorial team at André Deutsch for their expertise and encouragement, and in particular production master John Cleary, editor Zoë Ross, designer Donald MacPherson and typesetters Les Hall and David Caldwell. The authors also wish to acknowledge the co-operation of Thames Television in allowing publication of the transcript of the *This Is Your Life* tribute, and thank lawyer Henri Brandman for his diligence. Harry Carpenter was, as ever, a source of inspiration, particularly on the 'Here's Harry' chapter. Most of all, thanks to Laura for keeping Frank organised and making sure he was booked for this assignment.

PHOTOGRAPHIC ACKNOWLEDGEMENTS: The authors thank Lord Snowdon for permission to use his striking photograph on the front cover. The majority of the photographs printed in the two picture sections are from Frank Bruno's private family album. The authors also thank *The Sun*, *All Sport*, the *Daily Mail*, the *Daily Express*, *Associated Press*, McKenzie Clark Limited and *Thames Television* for their kindness in supplying pictures to Frank Bruno.

A Big Thank You

[signature: Frank Bruno]

I WAS standing under a large golf umbrella upstairs on an open-top London bus when it suddenly sunk in that my dream really had come true: *I was the heavyweight champion of the world*. So much had happened since the night I took the WBC championship from Oliver McCall that I had not had time to stop and think about just what I had achieved. At last I was on top of the mountain after falling off three times. Now, six days after winning the title, I was being paraded through London under a black, leaking sky on a bus that had been laid on by *The Sun* and Sky Television. In truth, I was a very reluctant passenger. All I wanted was to be at home chilling out with my family, and I was convinced nobody would turn out on a rotten day like this. I could see it being an embarrassing flop. Stop the bus, I want to get off!

But as the bus started on the planned route through the heart of London I was amazed to see that thousands of people had turned out to cheer me despite the pouring rain. Then it dawned on me. It was not just *my* championship. It was theirs as well.

There was no prouder person in the world than me as I waved from the top of the bus. I had come from these same London streets as the people cheering me and chanting my name. Bru-noooo. Bru-noooo. Yes, it was their title as much as mine.

This book tells the story of how I won the championship, and then put it on the line against the one and only Mike Tyson. To everybody who reads it, I just want to say a big 'thank you' for the part you played in helping my dream come true. Every one of my supporters gave me that extra vital push when the top of the mountain was in sight. It made me that much more determined to make the final step.

Now I shall pass over to Norman Giller, the writer who is helping tell my story. He knew me when I had zero, and before I became a hero.

Cheers. Nice one, know what I mean...!

Seconds Out
by Norman Giller

FRANK BRUNO has a funny effect on people. I have seen grannies stop and kiss him in the street, and grown men that he has never met before hugging him like a long lost brother. Children look up in awe at his six foot three inch frame as if he has just arrived from outer space, and ladies of all ages try to steal a cuddle. In nearly forty years earning my daily bread writing about sport I have never known anybody reach and touch such a large cross section of the public. The Prince of Wales looks on him as a friend, Lord Snowdon views him as some kind of black Adonis, his dustman, his milkman, his postman and his window-cleaner all consider themselves his personal pal. Priests, politicians, television presenters, plasterers, promoters (definitely promoters), photographers, physiotherapists, printers, plumbers, policemen, philanthropists, philanderers, publicans and publishers all regard him with great affection. Everybody, but everybody, seems to love Big Frank. He has a popularity that transcends boxing, and he cannot walk down any street in Britain without instant recognition.

But for all his fame, *who really knows Frank Bruno?* He has allowed only a handful of people to get inside his telescopic 82-inch reach, and he does his best to protect his private life from public gaze. What makes Frank Bruno tick? How and why has he managed to get under the skin and into the hearts even of people who think that a bolo punch* is some sort of exotic drink? These are among the questions we hope to answer in this book. It is the third collaboration between the pair of us. In our first two books, *Know What I Mean?* and *Eye of the Tiger*, I was the hidden orchestrator. Now I am coming out front in a bid to paint a proper por-

*A bolo punch travels in an arc. It was first introduced by Cuban boxer 'Kid' Gavilan, who based it on the bolo-knife action that he used when working on a sugar plantation.

trait of the man who everybody yet nobody knows.

When I have ghost-written for Frank in the past, his natural modesty has prevented me giving a totally accurate picture of a man who has hidden depths and who is much more intelligent and calculating than portrayed by his 'know wot I mean, 'Arry' utterances and his old *Spitting Image* puppet. Promoter Barry Hearn once described him as being as 'thick as two short planks' and had to pay out-of-court damages. Frank may not know his twelve times table but he certainly knows his value.

When I first met Frank he was a shy, suspicious and unsure eighteen-year-old building site labourer who was so broke that he used to try to dodge paying his fare on the London Underground. Sixteen years on he is one of the wealthiest sportsmen in the land, totally in control of his life, and he is that exceptionally rare breed: a British-born world heavyweight boxing champion. This is the story of what happened in between, and moving on to his headline-hitting return fight with the redoubtable Mike Tyson. We have covered Frank's early life in our previous books, and to make sure the picture is complete we turn to the transcript of his *This Is Your Life* tribute, which drew an audience of 16.4 million viewers. Frank and I thank Thames Television, presenter Michael Aspel, producer Malcolm Morris and director Brian Klein for letting us plunder the script which covers all the necessary family and schooldays background details, with some extra commentary from Frank inspired by the procession of guests from his past life.

Frank's conversational comments are clearly defined throughout the book inside glove-style quotation marks, while I concentrate on the navigating, as well as an occasional opinion and revelation that I have managed to get past Frank's defence. Part One concentrates on Bruno the man. The second part of the book is devoted to a fight-by-fight breakdown of Frank's ring career.

When Frank first showed me around his imposing Victorian mansion in deepest Essex, with its 117 acres, swimming pool, stables and private gymnasium, I reminded him that when we first met shortly after he had become the youngest ever ABA heavyweight champion in 1980 he barely had two pennies to rub together. Frank gave that deep-throat laugh of his and said: 'Yeah, I've gone from zero to hero.'

'That, Frank,' I said, 'will make a great title for our next book.'

So it's 'seconds out', and we start on the greatest night of Frank's life. He has just won the world heavyweight title. And he is in tears...

PART ONE
The Hero

1 : The Dream Comes True

*"I had dreamed and I had dreamed and I had dreamed of winning the world title, and at long last it had come true. They were the sweetest words I have ever heard "...and *new* world heavyweight champion, Frank Brun-o-o-o."*

IT had been a long, hard climb. Three times he had been within glove-encased reach of the top of the mountain, and three times he had fallen off. Or, more accurately, he had been violently knocked off; first by 'Terrible' Tim Witherspoon, then by 'Iron' Mike Tyson and, most agonisingly of all, by Lennox Lewis. Now he had finally reached the summit, and the tears rolling down his cheeks as the World Boxing Council belt was fastened around him were tears of triumph.

Even historic Wembley Stadium had not witnessed a night quite like the one of 2 September 1995 when Frank Bruno was finally crowned heavyweight champion of the world. The great god of television had demanded that the fight be staged in the early hours of the morning so that Americans could tune in to witness what they would have considered the formality of Oliver McCall regaining his championship. It was Mike Tyson who had once said: 'Good old Frank. He's our coconut. We American heavyweights like beating on him.'

But the spectacular pyrotechnics display optimistically organised by promoter Frank Warren and the Sky Television production team lit up Wembley with the news that, at last, Bruno was world champion at the fourth time of asking. It was not a classic fight (see page 180), but for Frank it was the fight and the night of a lifetime...

I have watched the video recording of the fight over and over again. I've usually played back my world title fights to see where I went wrong, so it's nice to see where I went right for a change. If I live to be a hundred I'll never know a night quite like that one at Wembley. I had dreamed, and I had dreamed and I had dreamed of winning the

3

world title, and at long last it had come true. They were the sweetest words I'd ever heard when American MC Jimmy Lennon announced: '…and *new* world heavyweight champion, Frank Brun-o-o-o.' Suddenly it was pandemonium in the ring. I wanted to drop to my knees and thank God, but there were too many people around me. If I'd gone down, I doubt if I would have ever got back up again. We've counted how many people were in the ring as the result was announced and it was over thirty, not including the security guards, photographers and television cameramen perched on the ring apron. My bottom lip was swollen and gashed and my eyes and cheeks were puffy, but I felt no pain. Just an incredible sense of relief mixed with pride and joy. It was the greatest feeling I'd ever known. It was *wicked*. I just could not stop the tears coming as I talked to Sky commentator Ian Darke. That was one part of the dream that was not quite right. No disrespect to Ian 'The Perm Man', but in my dreams I'd always seen my old mate Harry Carpenter holding the microphone as I told the world how I had won the title. But now it was for real, and to be honest at that moment immediately after the fight I didn't want to talk to anybody.

I was completely exhausted and just wanted to go home and cuddle Laura and the kids. I had been away from home for seven weeks preparing for the fight, and all I wanted was to be reunited with my family. I deliberately distance myself from them during the run up to a fight because I don't want any distractions, and the fact that I've not been able to see them helps me stoke up extra ammunition against my opponent. I convince myself that he has been standing between me and my family, and I take it out on him in the ring.

But I know that it's television that provides the corn, so I tried to find the right words for Ian Darke. I get embarrassed when I watch the interview. There I was looking like a bashed-up ET and trying hard not to cry like a baby. I have never felt so emotional in my life. I just babbled on, and it was my references to Uncle Tom that confused a lot of people. I was just trying to make the point that I was proud of my background and where I had come from. It was Lennox Lewis who was reported to have first thrown the 'sell out' insult at me, and Oliver McCall and the people surrounding him had taken it up. I think they just wanted to rile me up, and it worked. But I managed to use it against them. When I was feeling close to exhaustion in the last couple of rounds, it was the thought of the nasty things the McCall camp had been saying that helped drive me on.

There is no more insulting thing that can be said to a black man. To call him an Uncle Tom is to call him a traitor. I have never got myself involved in the black-white thing. I see people as people. They can be all the colours you find on a snooker table, but to me they are people. I'm very proud of my West Indian background but I don't go around shouting about it. I'm also proud to be British and am happy to wrap myself in the Union Jack. Live and let live is my motto. There's room for everybody.

Mainly I was in tears after beating McCall because I had managed to prove so many people wrong. Almost everybody seemed to lose faith in me after my defeat by Lennox Lewis, yet it was that defeat that convinced me I could *still* make my dream of winning the world title come true. A fighter knows deep down when he has the measure of an opponent, and I honestly believed that I was getting the better of Lewis in our title fight in Cardiff. Then I walked into his left hook and the rest is history. But I know how close I had come to knocking the heart out of him. I thought to myself, 'Everybody's saying that he is the best around and I've given him a tough fight, so there must still be a chance of me winning the title. I'll hang around a bit longer and see what happens.'

Everywhere I turned there were people telling me to pack it in. But I still had my dream. Nobody could take that away from me.

Confession time: I thought it had become the Impossible Dream, and I joined in the chorus calling for Frank to retire. Following his seventh round stoppage by Lewis, I wrote him a long, rambling letter in which I pointed out the special place he had earned in the hearts of the British public, and how he could damage it by continuing a career that now looked to be going nowhere. I was also concerned about the punches coming his way. 'You can build muscles everywhere but around your brain,' I told him.

Along with everybody else I underestimated Frank's desire and determination to become heavyweight champion of the world. It was not just a dream. It was an obsession. Suddenly he saw me as a negative influence, and kept me at a distance. It was nothing personal. He just wanted to have only positive thoughts as he plotted how he could get back into the world championship picture. He had an outstanding boxing teacher in George Francis and an exceptional fitness trainer in Keith Morton. Now he decided he also needed to train his mind...

If I had listened to everybody who was telling me to get out of boxing after the Lewis fight I would never have got out of bed again, let alone climb in the ring. My Mum was against me fighting on, and so were a lot of people whose opinions I respected. Dear old Harry Carpenter was among them, but I realised that he had my best interests at heart. Laura just said she would give me her full support whatever decision I made. But to be honest I never gave a second thought to packing it in. I was convinced that I could still win the championship. In the past Jersey Joe Walcott had won the title at his fifth attempt, so going by his record I still had two challenges to go!

I knew that I needed to pump myself up with only positive vibes and I was determined not to have any negative thoughts about retiring. Nigel Benn had told me how much he'd been helped by the television hypnotist Paul McKenna. I had met him at several charity functions, and we got on so well that I invited him to my training camp a couple of times before the fight with McCall. It was not for hypnotic treatment. I'd tried that in America before the first Tyson fight but it didn't work for me. What I wanted to do was to get my mind right as I prepared for the most important fight of my life. I knew that it was now or never against McCall. If he had beaten me that would have been the end of my dream and I would have hung up my gloves.

Paul specialises in motivating people, and has had impressive results helping them to become more successful in their business and private lives.

He made me focus on my strengths and appreciate the power of positive thinking. Big-time boxing, all sport for that matter, is as much about confidence as anything, and Paul was great at helping me to relax and to make the fight a mind-over-matter thing. It is called the mind game, and Paul opened my eyes to what could be achieved by having the right kind of thought processes and being properly focused.

I am also a great believer in the power of prayer, and am never shy to admit my leaning on God's goodwill. In the dressing-room before the fight with McCall I prayed for God to be in my corner, and I read the old Bible that my Mum gave me years ago. It is something I always do before major fights. Just before putting on my protector and shorts I covered myself in holy oils that Mum had passed on to me after having them blessed at her local church. Then, minutes before the call to leave the dressing-room, I took from the Bible photographs of Laura with my daughters Nicola and Rachel, and my six-month-old son Franklin Junior. I kissed each of them and made a silent promise to bring the championship belt home to them. It was my family I was thinking of as I left the dressing-room that had been used by the 1966 England World Cup winners. I was on the way to *my* World Cup final.

I had to walk down a ramp that had been set up by the Sky production team. There were flashing laser lights, dry ice, thundering music and an explosion of fireworks. Only when I watched a video of the show did I realise just how brilliantly it had been stage-managed. But on the night I was deaf and blind to it all. I walked to the ring wearing mental blinkers as I followed the Paul McKenna advice to be single-minded and to think positively. All I was thinking of was Oliver McCall and how I was determined to make him pay for all the insulting things he had been saying about me. He was all that stood between me and my world championship dream.

Nine years earlier I had walked alongside Frank as he made the same journey from the dressing-room to the centre of the Wembley pitch for his first world championship challenge against Tim Witherspoon. I was working as the publicist on the show and had been feeding him lines for a headline-hungry press. That, too, was an after-midnight fight to suit the demands of American television. But Witherspoon was a bridge too far for the relatively inexperienced Bruno.

Frank dramatically ran out of steam after starting like an express train, and was painfully stopped in the eleventh round by one of the more formidable champions of recent years. By the time he fought McCall Frank had matured beyond all recognition, both physically and mentally, from the 24-year-old first-time challenger, and he did not need any help with his punchlines.

The experience against Witherspoon made all the difference to me when I went into the ring against McCall. I had tasted the special Wembley atmosphere, and was now better prepared for it. That first time against Witherspoon was quite scary. The tension really got to me, and that was why I was drained of energy in the second half of the fight after getting the better of things in the early rounds. Tim was a terrific fighter, probably one of the most under-rated champions in the history of the ring. If he had not fallen out with Don King I am sure he would have been around as champion for several years. Yet I might easily have beaten him that night at Wembley. Tim admitted to me afterwards that I had hurt him more than he'd ever been hurt in the ring before. A lot of people had me just ahead on points going into that eleventh round. I remember us both throwing big rights at an identical time, and we both landed. Unluckily for me I was going forward and Tim was backing off, so the impact of his punch was that much harder. My legs wobbled and Tim saw his chance. From then on it was goodnight nurse. He started bowling punches at me as if he was Michael Holding letting go with bouncers, and his fists were bouncing off my head. After the fight was stopped in the last seconds of the eleventh, I was asked whether I had made any mistakes. I replied: 'Just one...I came out for the eleventh round!'

By the time I challenged McCall I had learned the sort of tricks of the trade that would have got me out of trouble against Witherspoon. My ring-wise trainer George Francis has taught me how to hold while clearing my head, and to keep close so that my opponent does not have room to get leverage for his punches. The Frank Bruno who fought Tim Witherspoon would probably not have got through that desperate twelfth and final round against McCall. But I proved I had learned to wrestle, smother and bully my way through a round. Not pretty to watch and not in the text books, but it can be very effective when your legs have turned to lead!

It was the night of the Witherspoon fight that I realised just what an impact Frank had made with the British public. It was in the early hours of Sunday morning when I accompanied him to Northwick Park Hospital close to Wembley for a precautionary x-ray on his swollen jaw. The hospital was buzzing with casualty business, mainly dealing with patients admitted after accidents on the way to or from Wembley. Frank was lying on a bed in a side ward having his pulse and blood pressure checked when there was a sudden burst of applause and cheering.

The curtains were drawn back to reveal a line of patients and hospital staff queueing up to see him. 'We just wanted to let you know how proud we are of you,' said a wizened little man. He had been hit on the head by a flying chair as a mob of spectators angrily reacted to Witherspoon's victory over their hero. 'For us, you'll always be a champion.' This brought another impromptu round of applause as Frank, his jaw swollen to twice its normal size, raised his arms in salute.

One chap with his leg in plaster was pushed forward in a wheelchair to greet Frank. He shook his hand and told him: 'I fell down the steps at Wembley and broke my ankle before you got into the ring and didn't even see the fight. At least you had the consolation of being paid for the state that you're in!'

Frank handed out more than thirty autographed photographs to the patients and staff. As he lay waiting for an x-ray (which revealed only bruising) I suggested to him that he should call a press conference the following week to announce his retirement. 'You don't want to go through this sort of thing any more,' I said. 'There have got to be easier ways of making a living.' Frank nodded his head in what I thought was silent agreement, but he had his own plans for the future, and they did not include hanging up his gloves.

I know I looked like the Elephant Man by the time Tim Witherspoon had finished whacking me around the head, but I had no intention of retiring. At twenty-four I knew that I had not even reached my prime in heavyweight terms. Witherspoon had broken my skin, but not my spirit. And I quickly got evidence that the public were still behind me. Les Eyres, a good friend who is sadly no longer with us, drove me home from the hospital at around five o'clock on the Sunday morning. When I unlocked the door there were already dozens of hand-delivered letters and notes on the doormat from well-wishers commiserating with me over my defeat. The count of letters, Telemessages and telephone calls during the next week shot up past the 5,000 mark. The Post Office did a great job getting the letters to me because some of them were simply addressed 'Frank Bruno Gymnasium, London' or just 'Frank Bruno, Essex'.

All but a few of the letters were wishing me luck and praising my performance. A handful of nutters wasted money on stamps to send me their warped views on my colour, my performance or both. From the first day that I started getting publicity as a professional I have had to put up with insults from bigots and people envious of my achievements. I always adopt the attitude that they are entitled to their opinions, however sick. I just wish they would keep them to themselves instead of sharing them with me.

I particularly remember a telephone call that I got from master athlete Sebastian Coe, who had been at the ringside to watch my challenge against Witherspoon. 'You have no need to apologise to anybody,' he told me. 'You performed with pride and courage and we all love you.' That really moved me, and just ten days later I was in Edinburgh for the Commonwealth Games cheering him on the track just like he cheered me on in the ring. I had gone to Scotland to outline my future plans at a press conference. I kicked off by telling the boxing writers that I was giving up boxing and moving to a monastery. Then, the joking over, I got down to the serious business of announcing that, despite all the advice that I should hang up my gloves, I was fighting on.

What a difference nine years later after the McCall fight. Frank left the Wembley ring in triumph with Elgar's Land of Hope and Glory ringing in his ears. He was not going to hospital. He was going home as WBC heavyweight champion of the world.

I could not wait to get the belt home to show it to my daughter, Rachel. It was a belated birthday present for her. She had been nine just five days before the fight, and it really cut me up that I couldn't be there to celebrate it with her. My eldest daughter, Nicola, had sat at the ringside for the first time with Laura. At thirteen, we thought she was old enough to handle all the excitement. I would never have allowed her there if I had not been very confident that I was going to win. My Mum had watched my contest with Witherspoon, but had vowed never to go to another fight after seeing me take a beating.

She stayed home praying for me. Mum does not pray for me to win, but for neither I nor my opponent getting hurt. Deep down, she does not like me boxing. When I telephoned her immediately after the fight, I said: 'I've done it, Mum.' 'Yes,' she said, 'and I've already thanked God.'

I must have phoned home a dozen times on the day of the fight. It helped make the time pass quicker, and each call made me more determined to win as I kept telling Laura, Nicola and Rachel that I would be bringing the belt home for them. And there was a six-month promise I had to keep for Laura. The day she gave birth to Franklin she handed him over to me with the words: 'Here's the son I've always promised you. Now win that belt for Franklin.' I vowed that I would, and it was the most satisfying moment of my life when I was able to keep that promise.

It was nearly dawn on Sunday morning by the time we got home to Essex, and neighbours had painted a message on the road that read: 'Bruno No 1 ... We Love You Frank.' There were already congratulatory cards and notes in our letterbox, and the letter count was more than 10,000 before the week was out. *The Sun* and Sky Television got together to give me an open-top bus parade through London and, amazingly, thousands turned out to cheer me despite the filthy weather. I was overwhelmed by the public reaction and it made me realise that everybody was as hungry as I was for the championship belt.

The first thing I did when I got indoors after the fight was to buckle the belt around Rachel. She took it upstairs and laid it on our bed while Laura made me a cup of tea. It tasted better than champagne, despite my sore bottom lip. We then went to bed and lay either side of the belt while watching a recording of the fight on Sky. I drifted off to sleep, completely, but nicely, exhausted.

When I woke up five hours later I wondered if I had been dreaming it all, but as I turned on my side to gaze at Laura there was the belt as evidence that I really had won the world title. My face was lumpy and aching, so I knew that I had been in a fight. I went into the nursery to collect Franklin from his cot and brought him into our bedroom. I lay him down alongside the belt, and said to him: 'This is for you, Franklin. One day you'll be as proud of your dad as I was of mine. And one day you will understand that I won this for you.'

Franklin giggled and gurgled, and started playing with the green and gold belt as if it was a toy. I laughed aloud because I had pictured this very scene in my mind time and again during the long build-up to the fight. It was all part of my positive thinking. Now I had proved that dreams really do come true.

Twelve months before his championship victory Frank, a Scorpio, had his horoscope read. He was told that during 1995 he would have a baby son and that he would become champion of the world. What was not written in the stars was how nasty it would all get before he tamed Oliver 'The Atomic Bull' McCall.

2 : Taming the Bull

‘Oliver McCall was right out of order. He can say what he likes about me, but when he starts insulting my wife that is personal. It made me more determined than ever to give him a good hiding.’

IN an earlier life I worked as a boxing publicist with masters of the selling game such as Muhammad Ali and Jim Watt, who used to know how to put bums on seats without resorting to gutter-tactic insults. Frank Bruno has always handled himself with dignity in the build-up to fights, almost offering a hand of friendship to his opponent. Oliver McCall was different. He approached his world title defence against Bruno with a spiteful outpouring of verbal abuse that presented both himself and the much-maligned sport of boxing in the worst possible light.

Somebody at some time must have tipped off McCall that he could almost literally get under the skin of Bruno by playing the race card. Perhaps it had something to do with Frank's enraged reaction when Lennox Lewis was alleged to have depicted him as an 'Uncle Tom' before their world championship showdown in 1993. Frank hit Lewis with a libel writ on the eve of their fight.

A lot of people thought it was a publicity stunt when my lawyer Henri Brandman handed Lewis a writ, but I was never more serious. I had heard that he had insulted me in the worst possible way by calling me an Uncle Tom, and I was determined to shut him up. We eventually settled out of court when Lewis insisted he had never said it, but I could hardly believe my ears when McCall started coming out with the same rubbish. Only he went further. He insulted my wife. He could say what he liked about me, but bringing my wife into it was personal and made me more determined than ever to give him a good hiding. McCall talked a load of nonsense about me turning my back on my 'brothers', and said the fact that I had married a white

13

woman proved I had abandoned and betrayed my people. He was not saying it to sell tickets but to try to needle me into losing my temper in the ring, a suicidal boxing sin. It was a stupid tactic on his part because all it did was make me even more positive in my attitude. He went further over the top by saying that he was going to turn me into a vegetable because of what he claimed my friend Nigel Benn had done to his pal Gerald McClellan. (McClellan had sadly suffered brain damage when stopped by Nigel Benn in a WBC super-middleweight title fight). McCall told the press, 'I'm here for vengeance. I am out for revenge for what Benn did to Gerald.'

I don't know whether McCall was speaking from the heart or whether he had been wound up to say these crazy things by his advisors. Whatever the reason, he completely lost my respect. I usually respect any man who climbs through the ropes, but – just as with Lennox Lewis – I truly disliked the man in the opposite corner.

Oliver McCall had become world champion in one of the great upsets of the decade when he stopped defending champion and hot favourite Lennox Lewis in the second round at Wembley Arena on 24 September 1994. He caught Lewis napping with a thundering right over the top of his left lead, and the British-born Canadian waved a wobbly goodbye to his unbeaten record and to his WBC belt that he had been awarded after Riddick Bowe had tossed it into a dustbin. McCall defended the championship against granddad Larry Holmes and then agreed to a voluntary defence against Bruno.

The moment McCall landed his right on Lennox's whiskers I felt a strange sensation that fate was working in my corner. I knew that McCall was made for me. We had sparred many rounds together before my fight with Mike Tyson and he used to eat my left jab as if he was addicted to it. We had got quite buddy-buddy, and he had seemed a nice sort of bloke. That was why it was even more of a shock when he said all those crazy things when he arrived in London for the fight.

McCall is shorter than me, lighter than me and not as solid a puncher as me. He suited me down to the ground. The only thing I had to be wary of was that sneaky right with which he had beaten Lewis. In my training build-up in Lanzarote and then at my favourite place of

Springs Hydro health farm in Leicestershire my trainer George Francis and I worked on tactics to, as George put it, 'nullify his right'. This involved a lot of movement to my right during sparring (and so moving away from McCall's right), and concentration on keeping my left hand high, guarding my chin the moment I had thrown a jab.

I want to give full credit here to the part that George played in making me the champion. We go back a long way with each other. I was a young amateur when I first worked out in the Kings Cross gymnasium where he was training world light-heavyweight champion John Conteh. I idolised Conteh. He had great charisma and style, and the beautiful car he drove and the expensive clothes he wore opened my eyes to what you could get by becoming a success in the boxing ring. George was a bit of a sergeant-major of a trainer, bullying his boxers into super-fitness. But I noticed that he did everything that he asked of his boxers. He would run with them, do a lot of their exercises with them and dive into freezing water to swim with them.

When I turned professional under Terry Lawless I had Terry and then Jimmy Tibbs as my trainer. Then, when Jimmy crossed to the rival Frank Warren camp after my defeat by Tim Witherspoon, George was called in. That was the start of the 'new' Frank Bruno. He helped turn me from a pussycat into a tiger. First of all he toughened my training routine, taking me on exhausting runs across Hampstead Heath which ended with brisk swims in the icy waters of Highgate pond. In the gymnasium he introduced me to his murderous medicine-ball exercises, hammering my stomach muscles until they were like a wall of iron. Then he worked on making me less of a gentle giant in the ring. He called on more than forty years of experience as a trainer, teaching me all the old-pro tricks that you will not find in any boxing text book. He showed me how to unbalance opponents by a nudge to the shoulder, how to push down on the opponent's neck at close quarters (a Muhammad Ali speciality), and how to hold, particularly on the blind side of the ref. I wish I could have called on this knowledge when Bonecrusher Smith and Tim Witherspoon were taking free whacks at me. If I had been more ring-wise I would have grabbed them and held on the moment the first of their swinging punches unhinged me.

This may sound like dirty tricks, but boxing is a dangerous game and you need the cunning of a jungle animal as well as skill to survive and thrive. The Yanks have been doing it for years. Think of great fighters like Rocky Marciano and Jake LaMotta. They were savages once the bell rang, and paid little attention to the rule book. Mike Tyson is another who takes no prisoners, but the Americans are the first to complain when visiting boxers use similar tough tactics. If you can't beat them, you have to join them or risk getting eaten alive by the harbour sharks.

Before George got hold of me, I was too stiff and rigid. But he taught me to relax, to conserve energy and to get that all-important bend in the knees for full leverage of my punches. He also stressed the importance of getting my head down in the clinches. When I parted company with Terry Lawless after the defeat by Tyson I retained George as my trainer and I owe him a lot for helping to make me a world champion.

Terry Lawless is my oldest friend, and it was he who first introduced me to Frank. 'Meet the young man who will one day be heavyweight champion of the world,' he said by way of introduction. Those were the days when Frank had zero. With perseverance and determination of super-human quality, Frank made it to the top of the mountain but Lawless was no longer in his corner when he arrived at the summit. They had what Terry called 'a divorce' after the Tyson world title fight in 1989. It was painful to watch from close quarters, but their differences were insurmountable. Frank was convinced they had achieved as much as they could together.

Very quietly, after the victory over McCall, Frank picked up the telephone and rang Terry for the first time since their split. He just wanted to thank him for all that he had done to help lay the foundations.

It is now a closed chapter between Terry and me. We had some great times together, but I wanted to stand on my own two feet and make my own decisions. I surrounded myself with a small but wise team, and was determined not to go the American way of having a large mob around me. McCall had an entourage of twenty-nine in tow, and Witherspoon had even more in his party. Muhammad Ali used to travel with as many as fifty or more on his back. All of them feeding off him. I just have George, fitness trainer Keith Morton, corner expert John Bloomfield, masseur Rupert 'Magic Hands' Doaries, and my brother Michael, who has always been there for me. Then there's my eagle-eyed lawyer Henri Brandman, and, most important of all, Laura. She's a miracle lady because she keeps me organised while also running the home and bringing up the kids. This is 'Team Bruno'.

Keith Morton is my fitness guru who has given me new strength and muscle power. He has made me much more supple and durable with a carefully planned fitness programme that I'm sure is as challenging and demanding as that followed by any sportsman in the world. Going right back to my schooldays I have always been a fitness freak, and I am positive that I have run more miles than any other heavyweight champion in history. Keith has introduced me to a whole new set of exercises and gymnasium disciplines, and I never get into the ring in less than peak condition. I cannot understand the boxers who let themselves go between fights. I go out of my way to train even when I'm not fighting, and like to think I will continue to keep fit long after my boxing days are over.

There was one other unofficial member of 'Team Bruno' on the night that he fought McCall. Nigel Benn, who had successfully defended his WBC super-middleweight title with a seventh round stoppage of Danny Perez in the chief supporting contest, got showered and dressed in record time so that he could lead Frank into the ring carrying a huge Union Jack. He then took a place in the second row at ringside, standing throughout the fight yelling encouragement, advice and warnings as Bruno battled his way to glory.

Nigel and I have a special bond, and it was a tremendous inspiration to me to have him cheering me on from the ringside. Even with all the noise of the crowd I could hear Nigel yelling to me to keep my hands up and to watch out when McCall was winding up for one of his big punches. We always try to support each other, and I was at the ringside when he won that dramatic battle with Gerald McClellan. The tragic end for Gerald overshadowed what a magnificent performance it was by Nigel, who was out on his feet in the first round. He showed he has a heart bigger than his head the way he battled back. There can have been few greater British fighters than Nigel in the history of the sport and I was devastated when he lost his title while I was in Las Vegas preparing for my return fight with Mike Tyson.

Nigel and I are soul mates from the same streets. We've come from a similar background and know that it's a minefield out there. We lead different lifestyles, but have a deep, mutual respect for each other. Our good friend Michael Watson was at the ringside to watch us both win our fights at Wembley Stadium, and the next day Nigel brought Michael to my home for a chat about my win over McCall.

Michael has been in a wheelchair since his defeat by Chris Eubank in a world title fight in 1991, and is a constant reminder of the dangers of boxing. He and I are old pals who knew each other as amateurs and used to train in the same gymnasium at the start of our professional careers. It was tragic what happened to Michael, and it underlined the risks we take when we climb into the ring. I keep a distance from the debates on whether boxing should be banned. My view is that you have got to be allowed to do what you want to do. Nobody holds a gun to my head and makes me get into the ring. I do it because it is what I am best at and because it's the best way I know of securing a good future for my family. There will always be men (and even some women these days) who want to box. It comes as naturally to some as playing the piano to others. If the anti-boxing brigade ever drive the sport underground they'll have a lot to answer for because all the safety measures that are being introduced will be ignored on pirate promotions. Boxing's been wonderful to me, and I could never have given my family the quality of life they are enjoying if I was still slaving on a building site.

The building site was one of Frank's work places before he got on to the first rung of the professional boxing ladder. But to find out how he made his first preparations for the challenge of the boxing ring we need to go back to school...

3 : Back to School

'They taught me so much at Oak Hall about how to handle myself for the rest of my life. It was really hammered home about how important it is to be polite and to respect other people and their property.'

N O portrait of Frank Bruno can be complete without a look back to his schooldays where the foundation was laid for the boy who was one day to become heavyweight champion of the world. With Frank as my chauffeur, we drove from Essex into deepest Sussex and back in time to Oak Hall school which had been set up for problem boys by the old Greater London Council. We arrived in Frank's eye-catching new Bentley, certainly more stylish than the Green Line bus that dropped him off there in 1971 at the age of ten.

Oak Hall is a sprawling Edwardian manor house looking out on to ninety acres of rolling Sussex countryside. It had been the estate of Sir Harry Oakes, who had been a close friend of Edward VIII in the days when he was still Prince of Wales and struggling with his conscience over whether to marry Mrs Simpson and surrender his right to the British throne. Sir Harry, a multi-millionaire businessman, was murdered in mysterious circumstances while at his sunshine home in Bermuda in 1941. Oak Hall was handed over by his family to the GLC to help underprivileged London children, and it was established as a disciplined boarding school by the time Frank became a reluctant boarder. His mother helped organise a place for him at the school after he had been expelled from Swaffield Primary School in Wandsworth for fighting with a teacher.

Frank could not have been prouder than an Old Etonian on this return journey to his alma mater as he gave me a guided tour of the now wound-down Oak Hall. 'Just look at that view,' he said, sweeping an arm in the direction of a magnificent landscape not unlike the one he is now creating for himself in Essex. 'Breathe in that air. It's pure gold. You don't get that in Wandsworth, man. Mind you, when I first arrived here I was so homesick for the streets of South London that I used to cry myself to sleep every night and I used to curse my Mum for letting me come here. Didn't appreciate the view and the air then. Thought I was in prison.'

He led me into a room with bunk beds, alongside each of which was a small wooden cabinet and a narrow wardrobe.

This was the dormitory where I used to sleep. Up every morning by seven. Wash. Clean your teeth. Polish your shoes. Make your bed. On with the school uniform and then down for breakfast in the dining hall. If you were a minute late for breakfast or did not keep your room clean and tidy you would lose privileges, like not being able to watch the football on television. That sort of thing. The more serious your misdemeanour – I learned that word very early at the school – the heavier your punishment. Being rude to a teacher or fighting other boys could mean a place on the work party. That was like hard labour. Sweeping the school grounds, helping in the kitchen, digging in the garden. If you kept stepping out of line, it was the slipper. Really hard on my black ass, man. If you still hadn't learned your lesson it was a visit to the office of headmaster Allan Lawrence for a lecture that would make you feel one-inch tall. He had a way of talking to you that was worse than any physical punishment. Didn't rant and rave. Just got through to you with good common sense.

There were about fifty kids at the school, including some real hard cases. I was bullied in the early days, but the bully boy was knocked out of us. Many of us were hyperactive and really took some controlling. They kept us on the go to try and eat up our energy. We did some academic work. English, maths, geography, history. But the main concentration was on physical education. That suited me! Lots of cross country runs, long hikes, football, cricket, swimming, rowing and horse riding. Everything but boxing. For some reason, the GLC didn't allow it. Too violent. Yet boxing is the best way to learn to control violence and to get disciplined. I'd been aching to learn to box properly since my Dad bought me my first pair of gloves at the age of eight.

We were joined by John Urwin, who had been Frank's PE teacher when he first arrived at Oak Hall. He is now headmaster of a specialist school in Berkshire, following the closure of Oak Hall. More than anybody it was John who pointed Frank in the right direction in those formative years when he was hovering between becoming a young villain or the sort of responsible, disciplined citizen that Oak Hall specialised in moulding from 'impossible' cases.

To see Frank and John reunited was like watching old pals meeting up rather than teacher and pupil. There was a special bond between them that had been forged by six years of working together at Oak Hall, first as enemies and then as friends. 'Frank needed a lot of sorting out when I first met him,' said John. 'He was a rebel who made it clear that he did not want to be at Oak Hall. We had our hands full with him. He was aggressive and troublesome, and we had what could euphemistically be called some runs-ins with him. Like a lot of boys from a West Indian background, he was misunderstood. At ten, he had the physique of a fifteen-year-old. Because he was so big, people expected him to act like an adult but he was just a boy in a young man's body.'

John set out to win Frank's confidence in a manner that was beyond the call of duty. He was one of just five teachers handling around fifty of London's toughest kids. 'I just knew there was something special inside Frank if I searched hard enough to find it,' he explained. 'I knew that I was winning when one day he offered to dig my garden. I wondered at first if he had some ulterior motive, and in a way he did. He just wanted to forge a relationship. I asked him to clear the weeds and he cleared the lot – cabbages, sprouts, just about everything that grew there. He was like a human bulldozer. But that was the day I knew I had got through to him, and from then on he started to settle at the school and he eventually became a model pupil.'

As Frank walked me around what used to be the Oak Hall sports field, his mind was suddenly flooded by long-forgotten memories of sporting glories away from the boxing ring.

This is where I used to play football and cricket. I used to try to bowl like Michael Holding. I could whip the ball in real fast, but my direction was not all that good. I was better at football. Used to watch Chelsea a lot on the TV in those days, and I tried to play just like Peter Osgood. But I was more crash-bang-wallop than his skilful style.

21

Scored lots of goals here. Got into the Sussex schools team, and John Urwin was pressing for me to go to Brighton, our nearest League club, for a trial. But even in those days I had my mind set on boxing.

I had joined Wandsworth Boys' Club before coming to Oak Hall, and it was there that I put on gloves for the first time. I can remember it so well that my eyes almost water at the memory. One of the trainers, a Mr Levington, had heard about my reputation for being a bully and he decided I needed putting in my place. He looked around for a boy to spar with me and selected his son, Gary, who was at least five years older than me but the only one about my size. It turned out that not only was Gary an experienced amateur boxer but also a southpaw, which meant that he led with his right fist and right foot forward.

Now in all my daydreaming of becoming the next Muhammad Ali it had never entered my head that you met 'wrong way round' opponents. I just didn't know how to handle him, and he gave me a mummy and a daddy of a hiding. His right jab hit me so many times on the nose that my eyes streamed water. I'm sure Mr Levington never expected to see me again, but I'd got the boxing bug and was back there the next night and became a regular at training sessions. I used to get a reminder of that first experience of pulling on the gloves when driving through London and spotting a certain policeman walking his beat. It was Gary Levington, who made a successful career for himself with the old Bill and regularly won the Open Police Boxing Championship.

The only problem I had as a member of the Wandsworth Boys' Club boxing squad was that there was nobody around at my weight in my age group. I had three contests – all against the same opponent, a big, strong white boy called Gary Hill. I won two and he won one. In my first year at the club I became National Association of Boys' Clubs champion, but it was a bit of an empty triumph because I got a bye in every round including the final! They just couldn't find anybody big enough to match against me.

When I arrived at Oak Hall I was always on to John Urwin about my love of boxing, and he devised a training programme for me. I used to run round the sportsfield with a bin-liner on me, and I used to sweat buckets as I covered mile after mile imagining that I was Muhammad Ali. John had seen Olympic judo star Dave Starbrook running in army boots, so I had a go at that. Then, to make it even harder, I would run dragging two large car tyres behind me. In the gymnasium I devised a routine where I would get my school pals to throw the medicine ball at my stomach. It brought me a lot of respect from the other boys. Nobody took any liberties with me, know what I mean!

But it became frustrating to be doing all this training without being able to box because of school rules. Then headmaster Allan Lawrence and John got me into the local youth club at Heathfield, and the leader, Mike Hannington, tried to get other boys to spar with me, but nobody was interested. I was so big for my age that it was almost impossible to match me. At last they arranged a bout for me down at Alan Minter's old club at Crawley, but when I arrived the boy I was supposed to box took one look at me and said 'goodnight nurse'. He packed his bag and went home. Couldn't blame him, I suppose. I was a total novice, but I looked as if I could handle myself. If I'd seen me coming through the door, I don't think I would have fancied it either.

It was in my final term at Oak Hall that I at last got my boxing career back on the road. There was a lot of local talk about a sixteen-year-old heavyweight called Paul McDonald, who was reckoned to be the hottest young prospect around. At six feet tall and thirteen stone, he was, understandably, finding it hard to get opponents in his age group. I read in the local paper that he would take on anybody, so I travelled to his club in Claygate, Surrey, to challenge him. I was frightened out of my life, and decided that the best way to fight him was to concentrate on the left jab that I had developed while shadow boxing in the Oak Hall gymnasium. I managed to outjab him in the first round, and then bloodied his nose with a left-right combination in the second that forced the referee to stop the contest in my favour. John Urwin and I were as happy as if I had won the world title. My dream was born.

Let me be honest here and admit that I have never got over that fear of boxing. It gets no less with experience. But conquering that fear is a victory that every boxer has as he climbs through the ropes, and that's why you rarely catch me slagging off another boxer. Just getting into the ring is a victory in itself. Any boxer deserves respect.

The one-dimensional image that Frank has created in public amuses John Urwin. 'There is much more to Frank than the character portrayed in the press,' he said. 'All that "know what I mean" stuff is just a defence mechanism. He likes his privacy. Always has done. He liked to be alone with his own thoughts at school, and all his training was done solo. He would spend hours in the gymnasium and on the sports field working out on his own. There are a lot of sides and depths to Frank that are rarely shown. Anybody who treats him like a fool is asking for trouble. He can cut anybody down with a clever remark.'

John was once talking about Frank on television and lost his train of thought. Frank came to his rescue by finishing his sentence for him. 'That was hardly the action of a thick person,' said John. 'He can think and act quicker than most of us.'

To prepare Frank for the outside world, he was given a series of mock job interviews in the headmaster's study at Oak Hall.

I remember it clearly. I was in my last year at the school in 1977 and I had been made head boy. My knees were knocking as if I was going for a proper job when I went to the study to be interviewed by one of the school governors, Harold Becker. 'And what sort of job do you want to do when you leave Oak Hall, young man?' he asked. 'I want to be a professional boxer, sir,' I said. Mr Becker tried not to look surprised. 'Quite so,' he said, 'but I think you should get yourself a career to fall back on just in case your boxing plans do not work out. Just bear in mind that to be a professional boxer you will need to be totally dedicated and determined. That is not a sport to approach with anything less than a hundred per cent dedication.' They were wise words of advice that I've never forgotten.

I didn't know it at the time, but Oak Hall was the best thing that happened to me (along with meeting Laura). They taught me so much there about how to handle myself for the rest of my life. It was hammered home about how important it is to be polite and to respect other people and their property. When I was a kid growing up in Wandsworth I learned the exact opposite while running wild in the streets, bashing up other kids and making a nuisance of myself. My poor Mum used to despair of me, and would say, 'Franklin, what is going to become of you? I just pray that the good Lord looks after you.'

I would not have been so wild if my dad had not been taken ill. He had my love and respect, but suddenly, because of diabetes, he was too sick to pay proper attention to me. He was a quiet, thoughtful big-boned man, who always talked common sense. 'Franklin,' he'd say to me when I was in trouble for beating up a neighbour's kid or something like that, 'just do what your mother tells you and you won't go far wrong. God gave you hands to be constructive not destructive. Now be a good boy or I'm going to have to give you a good hiding that will hurt me more than it hurts you.'

True to his word, Dad used to give me the occasional good hiding. He used to keep a curtain rod hidden in a cupboard and when I was getting out of hand he used to take it out and whack my behind with all the power of Gary Sobers hitting a six. I mention Sobers because he was Dad's big idol, and he used to spend hours listening to the radio Test commentaries and cheering on the West Indies.

Even after a stroke had meant that he was confined to bed he still used to find ways of giving me a whack with the rod. He would hide it under the bedclothes and then call me to his room. 'Come round this side of the bed, son,' he would say, making sure I could not bolt out of the door, and also so that I was on the side of his body that he could still move. Then he would suddenly produce the rod and give me a whack across the behind. 'Your mother deserves better from you, Franklin,' he would say. 'Do as she says or you will be in big, big trouble.'

But despite the whacks (that I always deserved) I never once lost my love and respect for my dad and it really grieved me to see him in such pain in his last few years. It used to be so hard for him to bear that when I was home on school holidays Mum had to show me how to give him his injections. If she was out on a call on her district nurse rounds and Dad suddenly cried out with pain I had to go and get the needle and stick it as gently as possible into his arm. That was the hardest thing I've had to do in my life.

A weird and frightening thing happened on the day that he died. I was in my fourth year at Oak Hall and was walking through the school grounds when I heard my father's voice. It was as clear as if he was walking beside me. He was crying and calling out my name. When I got back to the schoolhouse about an hour later, the headmaster summoned me to his study. He put an arm gently around my shoulder as he gave me the news I was dreading. 'I'm sorry to have to tell you that your father has died,' he said. 'You must look on it as a merciful release from his suffering. We have arranged for you to catch the next bus to London so that you can go home and help comfort your mother.'

When I got back to our home at 39 Barmouth Road, Wandsworth, my mum was sitting in an armchair weeping. 'I'm sorry, Franklin,' she said, 'but the good Lord has taken your father. He is out of his pain now and in the arms of our Father.' Mum and I share a total belief in God, and in a life hereafter. She had become a Pentecostal lay preacher, while I was christened and remain, like my Dad, a devout Roman Catholic. I went upstairs to my bedroom and broke down and cried as I said a prayer for my dad. He always thought I was something special. He used to tell me that if I put my mind to it I could make a success of my life. My brother Michael repeated recently what my dad once said, 'God's spotlight shines down and picks out certain people. You're one of the chosen ones.' As I cried in my room I secretly vowed to do something that would make my dad, up there in Heaven, proud of me. Really proud.

Robert Bruno, Frank's dad, would have been as proud as punch of his boy the night that he became the target for Michael Aspel and his *This Is Your Life* red book. The rebel schoolboy of Oak Hall had come a long way, as more than sixteen million television viewers were about to discover.

4 : This Is My Life

'If I had known what was being planned I would have run a mile. I just could not believe that Laura could keep a secret from me. But it turned out to be one of the most memorable and moving nights of my life.'

THE Frank Bruno 'hit' was planned just like a military operation. Somehow we had to get Frank in front of the *This Is Your Life* cameras without raising his suspicions. Laura, our chief co-conspirator, warned us that Frank would take some catching because he is such an alert character. 'It's got to be something really believable to get him,' she told the associate producer John Graham. 'If he guesses what's going on he'll run a mile.'

Having got Laura's reluctant go-ahead ('He'll murder me'), the *Life* hit team was called to a planning meeting at Teddington Studios by producer Malcolm Morris. I was present in my role as scriptwriter, along with presenter Michael Aspel, director Brian Klein, script editor Roy Bottomley, John Graham and researcher Sarah Cockcroft. This was in the second week of December 1992. The recording date was set for 26 January 1993, with transmission scheduled for the following week.

We had drawn up a list of possible guests, and it was reckoned that including Frank's relatives and closest friends there would be about seventy people on set. There would need to be relatives flown in from the West Indies, and we put in calls to the United States to see whether Muhammad Ali or Mike Tyson would be available to join us live at Teddington Studios. Our main concentration was on planning what is known in *Life* jargon as the 'pick up' or 'hit'. Frank was given the codename 'Glove', and from that first meeting until the day of the show nobody ever used his proper name. Security at the *Life* office is MI5-tight. Any hint of a leak and the show is dropped.

We explored several pick-up possibilities, including Michael climbing into the ring disguised as a referee, invading Frank's gymnasium and also sneaking in at the ringside while he was being interviewed by Harry Carpenter. We dropped them all because the security risk was too great. Finally we settled on bringing Frank's pal Freddie Starr in on the secret. They had recently recorded a *Freddie Starr Special* for Central Television, and Laura booked Frank to go to the London office of Central to see an unedited preview of the show with Freddie.

Laura told me that Freddie's producer had phoned to suggest that I should see the unedited version in case there was anything I wanted to change. He had also wanted me there, so Laura said, to have some publicity shots taken with Freddie. This struck me as a bit odd because when I was recording the show with Freddie in the Midlands there was a Central Television photographer taking pictures right, left and centre. But you don't stop and think, 'This has got to be a catch. They're setting me up for *This Is Your Life*.' So I told Laura to go ahead and accept the date. Freddie is a good old mate of mine, and I would not think twice about going to see him even though this usually meant non-stop leg-pulling. But Laura was right. If I had had even the slightest suspicion it was for a *This Is Your Life* programme I would have run a mile. I love the show when it's about other people but, believe it or believe it not, I'm a pretty shy man at heart and always felt I would have died of embarrassment.

Frank was sitting in the Central viewing room watching the screen alongside Freddie Starr when Michael Aspel made his entrance followed by two cameramen with hand-held cameras. Frank was concentrating on watching a sketch in which he appeared with Freddie. Suddenly he looked up to see Michael approaching with the Big Red Book. Frank was relaxed when he first saw Michael. He thought he must be there for Freddie. Then, as it dawned on him that he was the subject, Frank looked as shocked as if he had been hit on the jaw. He was speechless as Michael said the famous words: 'Frank Bruno, tonight This Is Your Life.' (*'I just couldn't believe that Laura had kept this secret from me. Freddie kissed me on the cheek and said, 'Gotcha, Big Man.' I was in a daze as Michael led me out of the Central office and into a waiting limousine. Even then I wondered if it was a wind-up by Freddie.'*).

28

This, with thanks to Thames Television, is the actual script of the show, with extra commentary in italics thrown in by Frank:

FRANK ENTERS WITH MICHAEL, KISSES LAURA AND HIS MOTHER AND THEN SITS SURROUNDED BY SIXTY CLOSE FRIENDS AND RELATIVES.

MICHAEL: Well, as you can see, Frank, you're topping the bill tonight with some special friends and relatives. Here along with your wife Laura are your mother Lynette, brother Michael, sisters Faye and Joan (Angela was unable to make it), and Laura's family, the Mooneys, headed by your in-laws Peter and Mary. And over here facing you, close friends and associates including your trainer George Francis, promoter Mickey Duff, your world champion boxing mates Nigel Benn and Duke McKenzie, together with former British heavyweight champion Horace Notice and your schoolboy idol, another world champion, John Conteh. Also here, of course, your comedy sparring partner, Freddie Starr.

FREDDIE ENTERS, CUDDLES FRANK AND STANDS.

MICHAEL: Freddie, thank you for helping us out.

(Freddie is not taking any notice of what Michael is saying to him, but is clowning as he mimes throwing punches at Frank.)

MICHAEL: Is there anything you want to say, Freddie?

FREDDIE STARR: Yes, I'd just like to say that Frank is a very difficult man to buy a present for. I bought him a Black and Decker for Christmas, and he's worn it out...

FRANK (laughing uncontrollably): Cool it, Freddie. This is a family show.

(For those who don't know, Black and Decker is rude rhyming slang ... and if you don't know, it's best that you keep it that way!)

MICHAEL: I take it that this is a private joke.

FREDDIE: Yes, very private Michael. What I've really come along here to say is that I wish to pay tribute to a truly great man...

(Freddie now has tears of laughter pouring down his cheeks...)

This man is a wonderful thespian...a true giant of the stage... and... I can't say any more... thank you...

(He is now laughing so much that he cannot get any words out, and he sits facing Frank with the studio audience and everybody on the set in uproar.)

(Freddie is a born clown. He always creases me up, and I don't think we've had more than five minutes' serious chat since we first worked together on one of his shows fourteen years ago. He told me later that he had wanted to pay me a serious tribute, but just couldn't stop laughing because of the Black and Decker 'in' joke.)

MICHAEL: That was a moving moment, seeing Freddie reduced to tears like that. Of course, Frank, you are not the only performer in the Bruno family. Here's your elder daughter, Nicola, earning a crust.

ON THE STUDIO SCREEN WE SEE THE POPULAR CHAMPION BREAD TELEVISION COMMERCIAL IN WHICH NICOLA IMPERSONATES FRANK WORKING OUT IN THE GYMNASIUM WHILE INTERVIEWED BY A YOUNG HARRY CARPENTER LOOK-ALIKE. BOTH MIME TO THE VOICES OF FRANK AND HARRY.

MICHAEL: Well, Nicola is ten years old now, and she's here along with your other lovely daughter, six-year-old Rachel.

NICOLA AND RACHEL ENTER, KISS AND CUDDLE FRANK AND THEN SIT BETWEEN LAURA AND FRANK'S MOTHER.

MICHAEL: The other voice we heard on that commercial, of course, belonged to the man who has become your double act partner...

HARRY CARPENTER (voice off): You got me to the Palladium, but we didn't get to meet the Queen... know what I mean, Frank!

MICHAEL: Your good friend, Harry Carpenter.

HARRY ENTERS, GREETS AND STANDS.

MICHAEL: Harry, what happened at the Palladium?

HARRY: Well, we did a cross-talk act in front of Her Majesty the Queen. As you well know, Michael, the people who take part in the show are later invited to go backstage to meet the Queen. You and I, Frank, got a good pitch in the second row behind an excellent South American group called The Gauchos. They had gone down a storm. Anyway, the Queen comes along with Prince Philip behind her and stops right in front of us and congratulates The Gauchos on their superb performance. Then she moves off, and she has not gone hardly a yard when Frank says with that booming voice of his (impersonates Frank): 'She's gorn and blown you out 'Arry.'

THERE'S A LOT OF LAUGHTER BEFORE HARRY CONTINUES.

HARRY: Can I just add, Michael, that this man is quite amazing. I've been around with a lot of famous people in sport in my time, and I have never known anybody get into the hearts of the nation quite like him. I know it's true because everywhere I go in Britain people are constantly stopping me and asking, 'Where's Frank?' And just one other thing: he's not a bad fighter, either.

FRANK: Thanks very much, Harry. You're a gentleman.

HARRY SITS ALONGSIDE FREDDIE STARR, WHO IS STILL DABBING HIS EYES WITH A HANDKERCHIEF FOLLOWING HIS ENCOUNTER WITH FRANK.

MICHAEL: Well, Franklin Roy Bruno, This Is Your Life... and you are born in Hammersmith General Hospital on November sixteenth 1961, weighing in at nine-and-a-half pounds. Here you are at the age of two with your mother Lynette and your late father, Robert.

(I had to fight to hold back the tears when I saw the photograph on screen of my dad. He was the most important influence on me in my early life. He had no luck when he came over here in search of the Promised Land that all West Indians were told about by the British Government back in the 1950s. He and Mum arrived with nothing, and they were prepared to work themselves into the ground to give us kids a decent start in life. It was Dad who bought me my first pair of boxing gloves when I was about eight, and he encouraged me to try to use my strength in a sensible rather than reckless way. I know that he would have been busting with pride to see me sitting in the This Is Your Life *seat.)*

MICHAEL: You are the youngest of five children born to Robert, a bakery worker, and Lynette, a district nurse, and you have another brother, Eddie, living in your mother's homeland of Jamaica. Your father was born in Dominica, and your parents come to England in the late 1950s and settle in Wandsworth. When growing up in Wandsworth, you are always head and shoulders above other boys your age and you are continually getting into fights. Lynette, this must have been very difficult for you because you are a Pentecostal lay preacher.

LYNETTE: Yes, Michael, but he was not a bad boy. It was just that within him was this natural strength for fighting. I remember one day I got a call from the Headmaster at the Swaffield Road Primary school that he was attending because Frank had been involved in some sort of incident. When I got to the school I found out that he had been fighting with a teacher...

FRANK: I was only wrestling with the teacher, Mum.

MICHAEL: We should, I think, make it clear that this was a male teacher.

LYNETTE: The Headmaster advised me that he could not keep Frank at the school any longer because his strength was more than they could handle.

(The teacher I had the fight with was a real flash bloke who kept showing off to the girls. We were out on a school visit to the House of Commons when I sort of borrowed a girl's camera to take a picture without asking. The teacher went for me in a really aggressive way, and we tumbled on to the floor in a wrestling match. I suddenly realised what a stupid thing I was doing, and I ran off as fast as my legs would take me across Westminster Bridge and all the way home to Wandsworth. It was the final straw for the Headmaster at my primary school because I had been wearing a hole in his carpet with the number of times I had been called to his office.)

MICHAEL: Your mother takes advice, and reluctantly packs you off to the Greater London Council-run Oak Hall school in Sussex where strict discipline is the order of the day...

A PHOTOGRAPH COMES ON SCREEN SHOWING FRANK AGED TWELVE WITH BUSHY HAIR.

FRANK: That's my Afro hairstyle.

MICHAEL: (battling through the laughter)...and when you try it on with the teachers here you more than meet your match.

JOHN URWIN (voice off): We had a few run-ins, Frank, but you settled down to become a model pupil.

MICHAEL: He was your PE teacher, now your friend John Urwin... and here with him Oak Hall headmaster Allan Lawrence, and his wife, Joan.

JOHN URWIN AND ALLAN AND JOAN LAWRENCE ENTER, GREET AND STAND.

MICHAEL: So, John, you had some altercations with young Frank?

JOHN URWIN: Yes, young Frank was a wild person when he first arrived at Oak Hall, and it was my job to try to channel all that power and energy into something good not bad. It's true to say we had a few confrontations...

FRANK: We sure did, sir...

JOHN URWIN: ...but eventually his performances on the sports field and in the school made him somebody who everybody looked up to. I think we can say quite safely that you became a model pupil...know what I mean, Frank!

MICHAEL: Allan, did you ever think that Frank would turn out the way he has?

ALLAN LAWRENCE: It was always on the cards. Frank had a certain aura about him, although in the early days it was not always an acceptable one. I didn't think when I used to wave my finger at him and tell him off that one day he was going to be a heavyweight boxing champion. He went on to become our head boy and sports captain, and then from school went on to his successes in the worlds of show business and boxing. Frank has quite deservedly become very popular, and I have never ever seen him try to take advantage of that. He's a true friend, and we are very, very proud of him.

FRANK: Thank you very much for all that you've done for me.

THEY ALL SIT.

(I can never emphasise too much what a wonderful foundation they gave me for life at Oak Hall. I was a real rascal when I first went there, but they knocked me into shape and taught me right from wrong and how to be dignified and polite. Teachers like John Urwin and Allan Lawrence are diamonds who make other people sparkle. It was a real thrill for me to have them on my This Is Your Life *programme because without them I might have finished up as some sort of villain, maybe a black Ronnie Biggs. I owe them so much, and I know they have done a lot to help many other youngsters. They're wonderful people.)*

MICHAEL: While boxing as an amateur you take a variety of jobs including plumber's mate, working in a metal polish factory, in the Lonsdale Sports Shop and on a building site. It was working on the building site that convinced you that you wanted to become a professional boxer. Is that right?

FRANK: Most definitely, Michael. I realised that you could make a lot more money as a professional boxer, and you didn't get frozen to the bone. It was Bruno do this, Bruno do that, Bruno go here, Bruno go there, Bruno make the tea. I thought professional boxing could only be easier.

MICHAEL: While boxing with the Sir Philip Game Amateur Boxing Club you win twenty of your twenty-one contests and reverse your only defeat by Irish international Joe Christle. At eighteen you become the youngest ever winner of the ABA heavyweight championship, outpointing Welshman Rudi Pika in the 1980 Final at Wembley. In your final season as an amateur you represent Young England, and are on the verge of boxing for the senior international team when you decide to try your luck as a professional. Now Michael, you're Frank's older brother and have always been a guiding light for Frank. You were so impressed by his performance in the ABA Final that you wanted to write about it.

MICHAEL BRUNO: Correct, Michael. I wrote in large letters on the kitchen wall at our home that Franklin would one day become heavyweight champion of the world. And d'you know what, champ, I still think you will. Good luck to you.

FRANK BRUNO: Thank you, Michael.

(Michael has always been somebody I look up to, and not just because he's a couple of inches taller than me! He has encouraged me throughout my career, and I am lucky to have him around when I need somebody to talk common sense to me if things are ever looking rocky. I am lucky to have a brother like him.)

MICHAEL: It looks as if your career is over even before it starts when you are refused a professional boxer's licence because of short-sightedness in your right eye. Terry Lawless, the manager who is to guide your career for nine years, sends you to Colombia for what was then revolutionary laser treatment that cures the problem. You start your professional career on St Patrick's Day 1982 with a first round knock out victory over American-based Mexican Lupe Guerra, and then make a name for yourself with a succession of quick victories like these…

ON THE SCREEN A RAPID SEQUENCE OF THE BRUNO STOPPAGE VICTORIES OVER RUDI GAUWE, GILBERTO ACUNA, EDDIE NEILSEN AND MIKE JAMESON IS SHOWN.

MICHAEL: Now Nigel Benn, as WBC world super-middleweight champion, you know a thing or two about the business. How do you rate Frank?

NIGEL BENN: Well, anybody who can wobble Mike Tyson can, I believe, go all the way. I know Frank has had two cracks at the title, but I think at the third time of asking he will become champion.

MICHAEL: I seem to remember that Frank was supporting you rather loudly in your last defence against Nicky Piper.

NIGEL: Yeah, well I can usually hear my dad above the crowd shouting advice and encouragement. But this time there was an even louder voice, and I knew it wasn't my dad because I know his voice. I realised it was Frank, who was yelling 'Use your jab…use your jab…' 'All right, Frank,' I said, 'I'll use my jab, I'll use my jab.' There was no way with Frank behind me that I was going to lose that night. Thanks for your support, Frank, and I'll support you all the way as well.

FRANK: Cheers, Nige. Nice one.

MICHAEL: There was never any doubt about the stunning power of your punches, Frank, but it was decided that your balance needed some improvement. An expert was on tap to help.

ROY CASTLE (voice off): You led me a merry dance, Frank, and really put your foot in it.

MICHAEL: It is, of course, the record breaking tap dancing master himself, Roy Castle.

ROY CASTLE ENTERS, HUGS FRANK AND STANDS. THEN HE DOES A SOFT SHOE SHUFFLE, WHICH FRANK TRIES TO COPY.

MICHAEL: Welcome, Roy. So Frank joined the Roy Castle school of dancing?

ROY CASTLE: It was decided that Frank needed some lateral movement to go with his front and back steps in the boxing ring. He turned up at the school with a baseball cap pulled down over his eyes so that nobody knew it was him, as if he could keep a low profile! He was quite shy about being taught to dance at first, but I soon got him doing this...

ROY DANCES FROM SIDE TO SIDE.

Then I was suddenly called away to the phone. I asked a young lad who was a good dancer to take over with Frank. As I came off the phone, the lad came past me in a whoosh. He was a very gentle lad, if you follow me, and he had said to Frank (effeminate voice): 'You're a good mover, Frank...you'll really look good doing this in the ring.' Frank, with that deep bass voice of his, said: 'Yeah, but there's gotta be a bit of this as well.'

ROY MIMES LASHING OUT WITH HIS FISTS.

That was too much for the young lad, and he ran past me like a greyhound with his tail on fire. But you persevered and stuck at the lessons, didn't you Frank, and now you can do the basic kick-step exercise known to all dancers...

ROY AND FRANK DO A KICK-STEP ROUTINE TOGETHER TO LOUD APPLAUSE FROM THE AUDIENCE. THEN ROY SITS.

(What a tragedy when Roy died the following year. He was one of the bravest men I ever met. Even when he was in agony with his cancer, he kept travelling the country raising money so that others would not suffer like he did. He was a record breaker all his life…with his dancing, and the way he faced up to approaching death. A giant of a man. He made me feel very humble and privileged to have known him.)

MICHAEL: Your boxing career is just beginning to take off in a big way when you meet your match on stage at the Shaftesbury Theatre in a Comic Relief charity show…

ON SCREEN, WE SEE THE HILARIOUS *ROMEO AND JULIET* BALCONY SKETCH. LENNY HENRY (IMPERSONATING FRANK) IS ROMEO AND FRANK IS A BIG-BOSOMED JULIET.

MICHAEL (indicating screen): And here is your co-star Lenny Henry.

WE SEE A CLOSE-UP HEAD AND SHOULDERS OF LENNY FILMED AT HIS HOME.

LENNY HENRY: They gotcha, Frank. (Laughs into camera and then impersonates Muhammad Ali.) Here's a little poem that I wrote for my good friend, Frank Bruno. (He now switches to Frank's voice):

There is a lovely man that you know,
His name, of course, is Frank Bruno.
When he climbs into the boxing ring
He can't wait for the bell to go, uh, ting.
He's criticised for doing pantomime,
But to be honest he has a wicked time.
It's a worthwhile fun kind of a job
And it beats getting smacked in the gob.
With his smashing kids and gorgeous wife
It's terrific that he's on This Is Your Life.
From me, 'nuff respect and more love than you can carry;
And, by the way, give my regards to 'Arry.
Ha, ha, ha.

(Lenny as himself): Have a fantastic time, Frank. Peace.

(Lenny and I have become good friends since that Romeo and Juliet *sketch, and Laura and I have socialised with Lenny and his brilliantly talented wife Dawn French. When Lenny first approached me about the Comic Relief sketch it was one of the funniest telephone calls I've ever taken, and you have to remember that when he contacted me I had never appeared on stage.)*

'Frank,' said Lenny on the phone, 'We'd like you to appear on next month's Comic Relief Show at the Shaftesbury Theatre.'

'Great,' I said. 'It will be a privilege.'

'You'll appear on stage with me.'

'Fine, Lenny. I look forward to it.'

'We're going to do the balcony scene from Romeo and Juliet.'

'Err...great. I did hear right. You did say Romeo and Juliet, *Lenny? As in Shakespeare?'*

'That's right, Frank. And I'm going to play the part of Romeo. And I'll play it as though I'm you.'

'Err...I see, Lenny. And dare I ask what you want me to do?'

'Well we don't want you to play the part of the balcony, Frank. So that only leaves one part. That's Juliet...Hello...are you still there, Frank?'
'You're not winding me up, are you Lenny. You really mean it. You want me to play the part of Juliet?'

'I'm perfectly serious Frank. It'll bring the house down. And maybe the balcony as well!')

MICHAEL: Thank you, Lenny Henry. Now in your early days as an amateur you meet Laura, and you're together for ten years before getting your friend, Father Tony McSweeney, to marry you. There's the bride and groom on the day that you brought Hornchurch to a halt on your wedding day, February the fifth 1990.

ON THE SCREEN WE SEE SCENES OUTSIDE THE CHURCH ON THE WEDDING DAY, WITH THOUSANDS OF ONLOOKERS BLOCKING THE STREETS.

MICHAEL: Laura, how did the pair of you meet?

LAURA BRUNO: We met at a roller skating park, and Frank was skating around posing. A friend bet me fifty pence that I wouldn't dare pinch his bum. I did, and I've been with him ever since.

(I didn't know it at the time, but that was the best day of my life when I met Laura. She was with me when I had nothing. Zero. She was a children's nurse when we first met, and used to help me out with money from her wages. When we first got together we started living in one room in my mum's house, and it was really tough when Nicola came along.

But Laura never complained once, and made loads of sacrifices to help me with my boxing career. She's a tough lady, too. She has kept it pretty secret, but for two years early in the 1990s she was in complete agony with what she thought was a back problem. Every specialist she went to see treated her for back trouble. Then one day it was discovered that her kidney was inflamed. She had a stone removed that was the size of a pebble. This had been the trouble all along, and it was discovered that her blood had become poisoned. She's clear of it now, thank God, but she went through agony without any moans or groans. Laura is a fabulous mother, and I couldn't ask for a better wife. She helps keep me organised outside the ring. If she had concentrated on a business career, she would have been one very successful lady. She won't take nonsense from anybody, and can be hard as nails when talking on my behalf. But underneath she has a heart of gold, and I consider myself very lucky that she decided to take that bet and pinch my bum.)

MICHAEL: In 1988 when on a family holiday in Jamaica the terrifying Hurricane Gilbert hits the island, causing death and destruction. You become quite a hero by helping to raise millions of pounds to repair the hurricane damage.

ON THE SCREEN WE SEE HURRICANE GILBERT CRASHING THROUGH JAMAICA, CLEARING EVERYTHING IN ITS PATH.

(That was the most terrifying experience of my life. Hurricane Gilbert ripped through the island at 200 miles an hour. The beach-side holiday hotel in which we were staying was shifting in the wind as if it were made of cardboard. As ceiling tiles and light fittings came tumbling to the ground I did my best to protect Laura and our two terrified daughters by gathering my arms around them and shielding them with my body. There was a load of rubbish written about me being a hero, but I only did what any father and husband would have done in the same circumstances. We were all in fear for our lives. I felt it my duty to help the island people try to raise money to repair the terrible damage that was caused. I was able to say truthfully to the press: 'Nothing will scare me after this. Tyson will be a breeze after Hurricane Gilbert!')

MICHAEL: Back at work you make gallant but unsuccessful bids for the world heavyweight title, first against Tim Witherspoon and then Mike Tyson.

ON THE SCREEN WE SEE ACTION FROM THE CONTESTS AGAINST WITHERSPOON AND TYSON.

MICHAEL: You widen your horizons and increase your show business work. You make your pantomime debut in *Aladdin* with Michael Barrymore at London's Dominion Theatre in 1989. Then you break all box office records when again appearing as the genie with the magic lamp at Nottingham, with Allan Stewart as your co-star. The following season you break box office records again, this time at Bristol in what you describe as the dark version of Robin Hood. Your co-stars are Little and Large...

ON THE SCREEN WE SEE FILM OF LITTLE AND LARGE TALKING IN A THEATRE DRESSING-ROOM.

SYD LITTLE: What d'you remember most about working with Frank?

EDDIE LARGE: His laugh.

41

IMPERSONATES FRANK'S DEEP LAUGH.

SYD LITTLE: Yes, but what do you remember about working in panto-mime with him?

EDDIE LARGE: His laugh.

EDDIE GIVES THE BRUNO LAUGH AGAIN.

SYD LITTLE: But you've got to admit he was a brilliant Robin Hood.

EDDIE LARGE: He was fabulous. Wandsworth's answer to Kevin Costner. D'you remember that archery contest we used to have to do every night, when we had to fire the arrow into the bull's-eye? I used to have a five pence bet with you before every show that Frank would hit the target. How much did I owe you at the end of the run?

SYD LITTLE: Twenty-two pounds, five pence.

EDDIE LARGE: What did Frank do when he heard about it?

REPEATS FRANK'S BOOMING LAUGH AGAIN.

SYD LITTLE: But it was great working with you, Frank. Hope we can do it again.

EDDIE LARGE: Yeah, as long as it's Maid Marian.

SYD LITTLE: Seriously, we wish you and your family all the very best, and have a great night.

EDDIE LARGE: Sorry we can't be there but we're working.

SYD AND EDDIE THEN GIVE THE BRUNO LAUGH IN UNISON.

MICHAEL: You were first attracted to boxing, Frank, by the exploits of the man you still consider The Greatest, Muhammad Ali.

42

ON SCREEN WE SEE A PHOTOGRAPH OF FRANK AND ALI TOGETHER DURING ONE OF FRANK'S TRAINING TRIPS TO THE UNITED STATES.

MICHAEL: Reg Gutteridge, ITV's Voice of Boxing, has this message from the man himself...

REG GUTTERIDGE (reading a letter from Muhammad Ali): 'Dear Frank, when I watch you fight I feel relieved that you didn't come along in my time. You might have given me a whole lot of trouble. I know that you're a good man, and have a nice personality. And you're not bad looking either. If we were matched for a title bout it would be awful hard for me to make myself angry enough to fight you.

So, Frank, I'm glad we never fought and I'm glad we'll never have to fight because I like you too much. I'll end with this little poem, just for you:

I'm no fool,
I've been to school,
And you're too cool,
You're not dumb enough to stay on the stool
and let me rule.

In all seriousness, Frank, I'm sorry I could not be with you for your special night. You are in my thoughts and in my prayers. Stay Strong. Good luck and God Bless. Muhammad Ali.'

(I will always rate Ali The Greatest, and it was a thrill for me to meet him several times on my trips to the United States. I idolised him when I was a kid, and had my ambitions fuelled by his 1970 'Fight of the Century' against Smokin' Joe Frazier. It's sad and upsetting to see him as he is today, a shambling shadow of the magnificent athlete he used to be. The boxing abolitionists jump at the chance to point at him as an advertisement for what boxing can do to a man, and they conveniently manage to forget to mention that the form of Parkinson's Disease from which he suffers afflicts thousands of people who have never laced on a glove in their lives.)

MICHAEL: Tom Shebhir is here from the Prince's Trust for which Frank is an official ambassador. And, Tom, you have another letter.

TOM SHEBHIR: Yes, Frank, I am here representing the Prince of Wales and I shall read out a letter from him at his request:

'Dear Frank,

I am sorry that I cannot be there with you in person this evening to give you a terrible shock and probably embarrass you dreadfully. But I did want to add my congratulations for this well-deserved tribute. I would particularly like to thank you, Frank, for all the hard work you put in on behalf of the Prince's Trust.

You have been an inspiration to many thousands of young people who have seen in you someone who from very modest beginnings has achieved great things. I can only salute you and give you my warmest best wishes.

Yours most sincerely, Charles.'

(Again, I was close to tears. Not because of the Prince's tribute, wonderful though it was. It was because just a few days earlier Jock Barr, a major driving force behind the Prince's Trust and a dear friend of mine, had died of cancer. He would have been the man sitting opposite me reading out the letter but for his death. I am proud to be closely associated with the Prince's Trust that helps underprivileged and deserving youngsters, and I am honoured that the Prince of Wales is kind enough to trust me with ambassador's work.)

MICHAEL: It was, of course, Prince Charles who presented you with your MBE in 1990. You often work for the Trust with another official ambassador, singer, songwriter, actor... Phil Collins.

ON THE SCREEN WE SEE FILM OF PHIL COLLINS SITTING IN A LOUNGE SETTING.

PHIL COLLINS: Hello, Frank. So they've gotch yer! Well everybody knows Bruno the Brute, king of the ring – one of our best-loved boxing champions. But what a lot of people don't know is the fantastic work you do with charity, particularly with the Prince's Trust. On behalf of all the ambassadors, the Trustees and all those kids whose lives you have touched just by being there and showing that you care about them, thank you very, very much. Have a good time tonight, and enjoy yourself at the party afterwards... know what I mean!

MICHAEL: Now something that I know you enjoy doing, Frank, is running. You cover an average forty miles a week whether or not you're training for a fight, and you have taken part in many half-marathons for your favourite charities. One of your regular running partners is a famous knight of the road...

SIR JIMMY SAVILE (voice off): Now listen, Francis, turkey legs would have been okay... but chicken legs!

MICHAEL: Who else, but Sir Jimmy Savile?

SIR JIMMY ENTERS, HUGS FRANK AND STANDS. HE IS WEARING A GOLD TRACK-SUIT.

MICHAEL: Jimmy, what has Frank been saying?

SIR JIMMY SAVILE: What he has been putting around about me is that I've got chicken legs.

HE DROPS HIS TRACKSUIT BOTTOMS.

Now I ask you, ladies and gentlemen, would you call these chicken legs? Next time we're out pounding the road together, young Frank, I will accept you calling me turkey legs but not chicken legs. I wish you good fortune. Thank you very much.

(Sir Jimmy is one of my favourite people. I have never seen anybody work harder for others. I remember him once inviting me to open a gymnasium at Broadmoor where he does a lot of unpublicised work to make life easier for the inmates of that sad place. Among the inmates introduced to me at Britain's top-security hospital was Ronnie Kray. Standing alongside him was the man known as the Yorkshire Ripper, Peter Sutcliffe. Seeing so many people locked up in Broadmoor was one of the most disturbing experiences of my life, and it made me appreciate all the freedoms that I take for granted. Sir Jimmy does not need to do all his charity work. He could put his feet up. But he is always looking to put something back into life, and I have tried to follow his marvellous example. I have to give Sir Jimmy the credit for bringing me to my senses about my

boxing career. After my third pantomime season he took me on one side and said, 'Francis, young man,' – he always calls me Francis – 'I want to ask you a very serious question and your answer could change your life. Do you want to be remembered as a pantomime fairy or as a champion boxer?' It was then that I decided to give everything to a campaign to become world champion. Sir Jimmy was a top-class wrestler in his youth, and had used the sport to help work his way out of the pits. He knew that I was aching to prove myself in the ring, and he found a clever way of making me motivate myself; to – as he would say – 'go for it, my son.')

MICHAEL: Together with Eddie O'Gorman of the Paul O'Gorman Foundation and Chief Inspector Mike Jackson of the Presidents' Sports Club you have helped improve the lives of many children like these...

ON THE SCREEN WE SEE A GROUP OF 60 CHILDREN FROM A SPECIAL SCHOOL FACING THE CAMERA. THEY SHOUT IN UNISON: We love you, Frank... Know what we mean.

(Another lump in my throat, and a quick wipe of tears from my eyes with a handkerchief passed to me by Laura.)

MICHAEL: In 1991 after a successful operation to repair a torn retina, you return to the ring as a self-managed boxer under the banner of promoter Mickey Duff. You have won your three comeback fights in some style. Mickey, can you tell us what's next on the horizon?

MICKEY DUFF: Provided Frank wins his next contest against Carl Williams, I will do my utmost to see that he gets a shot at the WBC world heavyweight title held by Lennox Lewis.

MICHAEL: And that, of course, will be against a champion for whom you have a lot of respect.

LENNOX LEWIS (voice off): I've got the belt that you want, and one day I'll give you the chance to try to take it off me.

MICHAEL: Britain's first world heavyweight boxing champion this century, Lennox Lewis.

LENNOX LEWIS ENTERS, SHAKES HANDS WITH FRANK AND STANDS. HE IS HOLDING HIS WBC BELT. THERE IS A DISTINCT CHILLINESS BETWEEN THE TWO MEN.

MICHAEL: Lennox, when can we expect you two to meet in less friendly circumstances?

LENNOX LEWIS : Well I've got my first defence against Tony Tucker, and I know that there have been secret talks between my manager Frank Maloney and Mickey Duff. They're hoping we can get it together in the summer.

FRANK (clasping his hands as if in prayer): Please, please I beg of you. Let's get it on.

LENNOX LEWIS: I will definitely give you the opportunity.

FRANK BRUNO: The British people want to see us in the ring together.

LOUD APPLAUSE FROM THE AUDIENCE.

LENNOX LEWIS: It will be a road block.

FRANK: You're right there. It will be a road block, and I can't wait.

(I know it was needed for the purposes of the show, but I was disappointed to have Lennox Lewis walking on. He had no real part in my life. But his cocky, arrogant manner just made me all the more determined to take his belt from him.)

MICHAEL: The last round, Frank, and I want to remind you of your first visit to Jamaica. You met your 84-four-year-old maternal grandmother Henrietta Brown for the first time, and you were distressed to find that she was losing her sight.
You organised it so that she could be flown here to London to have

an operation to restore her vision. It was the first time she had ever been on a plane. Well, now she's made the second flight of her life. She is here from Kingston along with your brother Eddie, your niece Edina and your nephew Jonathan.

FRANK WALKS TO GREET HENRIETTA BROWN AS SHE ENTERS, HELPED BY EDDIE (WHO STANDS TWO INCHES TALLER THANK FRANK). THEN COME YOUNGSTERS EDINA AND JONATHAN.

AS MICHAEL PRESENTS THE BOOK, FRANK HAS TEARS IN HIS EYES.

MICHAEL: Frank Bruno, This Is Your Life.

I could not hold back the tears when my grandma Henrietta came on. She was now eighty-nine, and it was fantastic to think she had made the second flight of her life just to be with me. Laura later told me that she had insisted that the *Life* team do their very best to get both my grandmothers over, but unfortunately my father's mother, who lives in Dominica, was not well enough to travel. It really hurt me just a week or so after my world title victory when a national newspaper tried to make it seem that I had ignored my Grandma Felicite. I will not drop down to their gutter level and discuss the story. Just let me say that my conscience is clear, and I will happily put up my record of what I have done for family members against anybody else's.

I was thrilled by the *This Is Your Life* tribute, although I found it uncomfortable at times when people were saying such nice things to my face. I had always wondered whether the subjects knew what was about to happen when Michael Aspel handed them the book. But now I know that they do not have a clue. Laura told me that she had been warned that if I got as much as a whiff that I was to be the subject, the show would be dropped. The element of surprise is so important to the show. Every time I watch the programme now I know just how the person in the 'hot seat' is feeling. You have a mixture of shock, bewilderment and, most of all, pride. Believe me, it's a tremendous honour to have Michael Aspel presenting you with the Red Book. Incidentally, the book that is given to you at the end of the show contains Michael's script and is taken back once the cameras are switched off. A couple of weeks later you receive a gold-embossed red book that is packed with colour photographs taken during the show and featuring the moment that you greet every guest that comes on. It has a pride of place in my home, and will always remind me of a memorable night when I was not ashamed to cry on television.

Eight months later a guest on the show was to give Frank one of his unhappiest moments in the ring and one of his most upsetting outside it. He and Lennox Lewis were going to 'get it on'.

5 : The Night I Got Lennox-ed

'Lennox Lewis is Canadian through and through. He was educated in Canada, was taught to box there, and won an Olympic gold medal wearing a Canadian vest. Then suddenly he was telling everybody he was British.'

NOBODY bugs Frank Bruno more than Lennox Lewis. It has always been Frank's contention that Lewis has used the Union Jack as a flag of convenience, and it infuriated him when he banged the true-Brit drum leading up to their world championship showdown at the Welsh National Stadium in Cardiff in the early autumn of 1993. Just how British *is* Lewis? These are some background facts that I gathered for a *This Is Your Life* tribute that was never paid. A dramatic right hand punch thrown by Oliver McCall led to a postponement of the planned programme. He was born in Stratford in East London on 2 September 1965, four years after Frank's birth fifteen miles away in West London. He moved to Kitchener, Ontario, when he was six to be with his Jamaican mother, then returned to Stratford and a succession of schools before finally settling in Canada at the age of twelve. While back in London he had close links with Rupert Doaries, a Jamaican-born former swimming instructor. By pure co-incidence, Rupert was several years later to become Bruno's faithful masseur who every day has hands-on experience of helping to keep Frank's spectacularly muscular body in supple shape.

Lewis studied at Cameron Heights, a high school in Kitchener that specialised in a sports-based curriculum. He set a school record in the javelin, and was a star of the basketball and grid-iron teams. But it was boxing that took his main concentration after being coached at the Kitchener police gymnasium by Arnie Boehm, who took him under his wing. He competed for Canada in the 1984 Olympics in Los Angeles where he was outpointed in the second round by eventual champion Tyrell Biggs. Two years later he won the Commonwealth Games gold medal in Edinburgh, and then reached the pinnacle by winning the Olympic super-heavyweight gold in the 1988 Seoul Games. He stopped American favourite Riddick Bowe in the second round in the final, and he received a local hero's welcome home on his return to Kitchener. The mayor designated 10 October 1988 Lennox Lewis Day.

Nearly every major manager in the United States and Canada was keeping track of Lewis, and the boxing world was astounded when he elected to sign for little-known London manager Frank Maloney, who had put together a package with the support of the Roger Levitt Group. The boxing moguls of North America were even more amazed when it was announced that Lewis would launch his career in England. He made his debut with a second round knockout victory over Al Malcolm on 27 June 1989 at London's Royal Albert Hall. This had been the venue for Frank's bow as a professional seven years earlier. By the time of Lewis's entry into the professional ranks Frank had fought thirty-five times. His last fight had been the world championship defeat by Mike Tyson. Now there was a young pretender to his previously unchallenged role as the uncrowned king of British heavyweights.

Lewis is, in my view, Canadian through-and-through. He should be proud of it, particularly after what he achieved for them in the Olympics. They gave him a hero's welcome home, but from the moment he turned professional under the influence of Frank Maloney he was suddenly giving it the proud-to-be-British bit. I wonder what all those Canadians who cheered him on in the Olympics in his Canadian vest thought of it when he decided he was British after all? I'd have had a lot more respect for him if he had been up front about what he owed to Canada. He was educated there, was taught to box there and he stood on the winner's rostrum at the Olympics proudly listening to the Canadian national anthem. Now he wanted us to believe he was British, seeming to me to turn his back on the country that had helped make him. You only have to listen to him talk with that Canadian twang to know his background. If he truly loves Britain, as he claims, why does he not spend more time here?

Lewis will always claim that he was the first British boxer this century to win the world heavyweight title, conveniently forgetting that he did not win it in the ring where it really counts. He picked the WBC championship belt out of the dustbin after Riddick Bowe had thrown it away. The belt was awarded to him by the World Boxing Council. Men in suits. He did not win it in the ring. Lewis beat an over-the-hill Razor Ruddock in an eliminator, and that was considered good enough for him to be crowned WBC champion after Bowe had decided he did not want to defend it.

That went against an unwritten rule of boxing: that a champion should only win or lose his championship in the ring. I agree that it was an impressive performance against Ruddock, but most people forget that leading up to the fight Razor was involved in two real wars with Mike Tyson that knocked the granny out of him. At least I had the satisfaction of winning the title in the ring. The fact that it was against Oliver McCall, the fighter who had stopped Lewis in two rounds, made it all the sweeter. That is something I will always have over him. Wicked!

Frank was convinced he could beat Lewis. I have never known him so confident and so pumped-up before a fight as when challenging Lewis for the WBC championship. Everybody was writing him off, but Frank kept insisting that the champion was over-rated and that he could beat him. He was not saying it to sell tickets. He truly believed it.

They swapped insults leading up to the fight that went way beyond the usual ticket-selling hype, and it was obvious that they genuinely did not like each other. Frank was steaming over Uncle Tom comments that Lewis was supposed to have made to journalists on the other side of the Atlantic, something which he later vehemently denied. Now Frank was out to ram the words down his throat in the unlikely setting of Cardiff Arms Park, ancestral home of Welsh rugby.

The Lewis camp deliberately chose Cardiff because they felt Wembley would be too much like giving me home advantage. But the Welsh fans got behind me just like they do in England, and they gave me tremendous support. I was adopted as 'Bruno Boyo'! There were a lot of people saying they were mad to put the fight on in the open air in Cardiff in October. But the promoters would not listen. We got half the crowd size the contest would have drawn in London, and the weather was unbelievably bad. Our final training in Cardiff was during the coldest September recorded in Wales for forty years, and the week leading up to the fight was one of the wettest I had ever known. A postponement seemed likely, but they decided that a canopy over the ring would keep the rain out. The fight would only be called off if the rain started to slant in instead of coming down in stair rods! It was one crazy night.

The rules were explained to us by referee Mickey Vann, and included with the usual 'break when I tell you' instruction was the addition that if the fight had to be stopped because of rain in the first three rounds it would be declared a no-contest; if rain forced a stoppage after four rounds the decision would go to the scorecards of the judges. It was a freaky way to go into a fight of such importance, but it was just as aggravating for Lewis as for me.

I felt sorry for the Welsh organisers because they tried so hard to put on a spectacular show, but the weather was their enemy. They staged the weigh-in at Cardiff Castle the day before the fight, and it bucketed down. The trumpeters from the Royal Regiment of Wales were all done up in their parade uniforms, but didn't get the signal for their fanfare; and a town crier who could shout the house down bellowed at the top of his voice, 'the heavyweight champion of the world, *Leon* Lewis'!

The rain eased off just before the fight that was scheduled to start at 1 am for the benefit of American television, and a change of canvas meant there was no danger of us losing our footing as had happened with several boxers in the preliminary contests.

It turned out to be one of the saddest nights of my life. I was in a positive frame of mind and completely focused on winning, and for six rounds I convinced most people in the stadium – including, I believe, Lewis – that I was the better man. I was continually beating him to the punch, and he was eating my left jab. Two of the American judges somehow had us even, but most ringsiders agreed with the scorecard of Welsh judge Adrian Morgan, who had me leading by a commanding four points at 59–55 going into the seventh round.

I was more than holding my own in the seventh, and I had Lewis backed up against the ropes under attack when suddenly he caught me with a flashing left hook. Full credit to Lennox. It was a cracking punch to produce when under such pressure. I was suddenly doing my stiff-as-a-board dummy act, and for the first time in the fight Lewis got right on top. His tactics did him no credit. He was holding my head with his left hand and then whacking me with his right. Referee Mickey Vann stepped in between us, and we both thought he was stopping the fight. But he was warning Lewis about holding and hitting. I had no time to recover and was still feeling dazed from the left hook. Lennox quickly came back at me firing away with both fists and I could not complain when the ref stopped it.

I was devastated, not so much by the punches as the fact that I had lost a fight I was certain I could win. That was the hardest defeat I have ever had to swallow...and it was a horrible taste.

Everybody was now telling Frank that enough was enough, and that he should hang up his gloves and enjoy the fruits of his hard labour. But the *real* Frank Bruno is not the soft, gentle giant that he has been presenting to the public all these years. Underneath, he is a stubborn and self-motivated character who knows his own mind but not his limits. The cheerful clown of the pantomime stage can sink into sullen moods away from the roar of the crowd, and he privately agonised over his defeat by Lewis. Out of his morose mood came a deep resolve to prove everybody wrong with what was almost a form of self-hypnosis. While the obituary writers were penning the end to his career, he was quietly making plans for a fourth challenge for the world championship. His dream had not died. It had been given new life.

Only in boxing could you get the irony that within two years of his defeat by Lewis, Bruno – the man they had all written off – was wearing the WBC belt, and Lewis was the ex-champion after a sensational defeat by a boxer who Bruno had been employing as a sparring partner: Oliver McCall.

When Lewis took the fight with McCall, I contacted Oliver who I then considered a friend. I told him that the way to beat Lewis was to pop his right over Lewis's sometimes lazy left lead. Sure enough, that's exactly what he did, and I was not that surprised by his victory.

I knew enough about McCall to realise that he was not the push-over that Lewis was expecting when he took the fight. Lennox was not properly focused on the McCall contest. I keep using that word 'focus' because it has become so important in my approach to fights. Lewis was thinking ahead to a match with Riddick Bowe, and he forgot the old boxing saying that you should take one fight at a time. I knew from the relaxed way he approached the ring for his defence against McCall that he had not got himself in the right frame of mind. It was almost as if he was going through the motions, and that is a dangerous mood in which to get into the ring against a serious puncher like McCall.

I could not believe it when Lewis's mouthy trainer Pepe Correa told Lennox just before the start of the second round, 'I want you to go out there and knock this bum out.' It just added to his relaxed state of mind and his thinking that this was just another easy job. He paid for it when McCall exploded his right hand on to his jaw in the second round.

Not surprisingly, Pepe Correa – the man who had loudly told George Francis that he would be out of work following my fight with Lewis – was no longer in the Lewis corner when he started his comeback after losing the title. I bet Lennox will never again make the mistake of not being focused.

While Bruno was busy taking over as champion from McCall, Lewis was battling for rehabilitation. He won an eliminator against Lionel Butler, and impressively stopped American 'white hope' Tommy Morrison in six rounds. Then he demanded a re-match with Bruno for the WBC championship. When it was clear that Frank preferred to put his title on the line against Mike Tyson, the Lewis camp took their claims for a championship fight into the courtroom. They went to the extreme of attaching a writ to the gate of Frank's Essex mansion. But the case was kicked out by the High Court judge, who ruled that the World Boxing Council, which is a Puerto Rican corporation with its head office in Mexico, fell outside the jurisdiction of British law.

I could have saved Lennox all that money he paid out to the lawyers. Tyson was the man I wanted, and there was no way I was going to fight Lewis ahead of him. I am a *professional* boxer, and it did not take an accountant to point out that it made much better business sense for me to defend the title against Tyson. He was the nugget of gold, while Lewis was just a grain of sand on the beach. I could make at least twice the money fighting Tyson that I could against Lewis. Boxing purists might shudder at that remark, but you have to face facts and accept that boxing is all about getting as much money as you can while you can. It's too risky a business to do it for fun. I know that Lennox would have done exactly the same thing in my boots.

Right the way through history champions, particularly heavyweight champions, have been allowed to make a voluntary first defence of their title against a selected opponent. Jack Dempsey, for instance, chose Billy Miske. Joe Louis took on Tommy Farr. Floyd Patterson went for Tommy Jackson. George Foreman's first defence was against Joe Roman, who they say that even Joe Roman had not heard of! And Larry Holmes took no chances by defending the title against Spain's Alfredo Evangelista. It was not as if I had chosen a push-over in agreeing to take on Mike Tyson, who was the World Boxing Council's official number one contender. Lewis would have to wait his turn.

There was an underlying reason for Frank's confidence in calling the tune as champion. He had impressive new muscle in his corner. Bruno had formed an alliance with a man who had re-established himself as one of the most influential figures in the world of boxing, Frank Warren.

6 : Warren Peace

Frank Warren had been written off after all his troubles a few years ago, and he saw me being written off when I was beaten by Lewis. We have both had the satisfaction of proving a lot of people wrong.

FRANK WARREN almost literally came back from the dead to pump life not only into his own career but also that of Frank Bruno. The two Franks formed a surprise alliance nearly five years to the day since Warren had been gunned down outside an East London boxing hall. They achieved their priority target within ten months: that elusive world heavyweight crown.

It was on a November night in 1989 that Warren had been left for dead by a would-be assassin, who fired a 9mm bullet into him at close range as he walked from his Bentley to a Barking theatre where he was promoting a small-hall boxing show. While Warren battled for his life in hospital, his suddenly rudderless business empire ran into a huge financial crisis during what was the crest of the slump in the recession. Frank Warren Promotions was suddenly on the point of collapse with debts of more than £3 million.

'It is worse than being shot,' said Warren, whose sharp Cockney humour was a main ingredient that kept him on the right side of sanity during a nightmarish twelve months. He told visitors to his hospital bedside that he had received a telegram from the Pope, who had survived an assassin's bullet. As eyebrows were raised, he would reduce them to laughter by adding: 'All it said was, "Hurts, don't it".' He discharged himself from hospital weeks earlier than expected (minus half a lung) to try to salvage his critically damaged business, and he looked the slimmest he had been since his teenage years. 'I can highly recommend the lead-plan diet,' he said. It could all have come from a well-scripted comedy, but Warren did not have a lot to laugh about.

Sensationally, it was Terry Marsh – a boxer who Warren had steered to the world light-welterweight title – who was charged with his attempted murder. Marsh was acquitted after a court case in which Warren's reputation was squeezed through the wringer as if he was the perpetrator of the crime rather than the victim.

He had to start again virtually from scratch after losing the position he had created for himself as a rival to even the long-established Mickey Duff-Jarvis Astaire-Terry Lawless team as Britain's premier boxing promoter. It was the second time he had started from the bottom.

Born in what was then the tough Arsenal territory of Islington in North London in 1952, this son of a bookmaker left school at fifteen to work as a meat porter at Smithfield Market. He then took a job as a salesman in the vending-machine business, and realised he had a natural gift for promoting any product he was commissioned to sell. Warren had been a boxing fan since he was a schoolboy, and indulged his love of the sport by bringing some sense of order and near respectability to the shadowy world of unlicensed boxing. His pirate promotions were presented with a style and a flair that appealed to the boxing public. He made several attempts to become 'legitimate' before the establishment finally gave way. Warren became a licensed British Boxing Board of Control manager and then, after using legal muscle to support him, he was given the go-ahead to promote.

He talked enthusiastically of building a much-needed indoor stadium in a capital city woefully short of suitable facilities, with most of his listeners nodding in agreement while silently dismissing it as a daydream. But it was not castles in the air for Warren. He provided bricks to go with his dream by putting together a consortium that raised £25 million for the erection of the London Arena in London's Docklands. Warren had shown he had what many creative people lack: drive to go with his imagination. On the evidence of all that he had achieved, you would be forgiven for expecting Warren to be a loud, swaggering type who likes centre stage. Far from it. He is surprisingly quiet and gracious, and he gives the impression of being almost shy. It is easy to be misled by his friendly manner into thinking that this is much too soft a man to survive in the piranha bowl that is the fight game, but a procession of reporters, publishers and critics can vouch that he has a vicious bite. He is quick on the draw with litigation and has had a string of libel successes in and out of court.

Warren is full of surprises, both in his business and private life. He is equally at home talking about art and antiques as he is about the records of boxers, and he puts his hand in his own pocket to sponsor promising but impoverished artists. His collection of paintings and illustrations of boxers, both old time and modern, is worth thousands of pounds.

There is a steely determination deep inside him that has won the grudging respect even of his sworn enemies in the always war-torn world of professional boxing. Most people wrote Warren off after the combination of his attempted murder and the torpedoing of his business empire left him like a battered boxer helpless on the ropes. But slowly he dragged himself back into the fight, and – with the vital infusion of ITV money – he re-established himself as a force in the fight game, even after he was barred as serving as a company director for seven years. Warren had three clever tricks up his sleeve. He gave himself instant muscle by forming a partnership with America's notorious Mr Boxing, Don King. This, coupled with a multi-million pound transfer from ITV to Sky, turned him almost overnight into Europe's premier promoter. In between, he linked up with Frank Bruno at a time when most people considered the boxer washed up as a world force.

Frank Warren and I got together when I was feeling frustrated after a nightmare trip to Hong Kong. I went out there in October 1994 for a fight against former Olympic champion Ray Mercer. Leading American promoter Bob Arum and British-born Oscar-winning film producer John Daly were the men behind the show, and Barry Hearn had his WBO champion Herbie Hide top of the bill in a title defence against Tommy Morrison. The master plan was that I would fight Hide for the title the following spring provided we both won in Hong Kong. Steve Collins and Billy Schwer were also due to have title fights on what on paper looked an exciting bill. Trouble was that few people in Hong Kong had heard about the show, and those that had did not seem to want to put their hands in their pockets. When we got out there after months of training, we found that few tickets had been sold and the show collapsed because there was not enough money to pay the fighters.

I have never been so angry as when I was told that the show was off. All the boxers on the bill had been treated like cattle. Nobody had bothered to consult us. We were only the fighters, after all. It was disgraceful the way we were ignored. They did not pull the plug until several of us were stripped for the weigh-in. By then a lot of British supporters had arrived, and were as stunned as us when they were told the show had been cancelled. The headlines in the newspapers at home summed it all up: Hong Kong Pong! My proposed title fight with Herbie Hide went out of the window with the break down of the show. A pity, because I am convinced that Herbie would have had just as much trouble against me as he did when losing the title to Riddick Bowe. But I would say that, wouldn't I!

It was soon after the farce in Hong Kong that I decided I needed a new direction in my career. I ended my arrangement with Mickey Duff, who had been involved in every one of my fights from day one. Mickey, and his partners Jarvis Astaire and Terry Lawless, had done me proud over the years, but I felt that I had gone as far as I could with them. I was thirty-three, and at the stage in my career when I needed to go forward quickly or not at all. This was the mood I was in when Frank Warren and I had a long chat. Boxing is only a village world, and so I had known about Frank for years, but without *really* knowing him. For much of his time in boxing, he had been an unwelcome rival to Mickey, Jarvis and Terry. But I had not got involved in the poison of politics. That's the one part of boxing that I despise. There is too much of this faction not talking to that faction, and ignoring this one or that one. I like to be on good terms with everybody, and have no time for all that like-or-hate rubbish. I take people as I find them, and as far as I am concerned Frank Warren has proved himself the right man at the right time for me.

I was first really aware of Frank when he used to come to watch my fights with Joe Bugner in tow, and throwing out challenges and making a lot of noise on Joe's behalf. That was when he first showed that he really meant business in the promoting game. He frightened the life out of the other promoters, I can tell you. It was a masterstroke to bring back old Joe, who first made it big, like me, with the Duff-Astaire team. Joe proved to be a drawing card with the public, and he opened the doors for Frank to get really established with ITV. It's no good being a promoter these days without the support of television. You've got to have your show on the box, or risk losing money. It was Frank's association with Don King that helped him open even more important doors because King has the American heavyweight scene pretty much under his control.

Frank had a lot of sympathy for me after my defeat by Lennox Lewis. He knew what it was like to be written off after all his troubles a few years ago, and he saw me being written off when Lewis stopped me. We have both had the satisfaction of proving a lot of people wrong.

I have never come across anybody to match Frank for attention to detail. He studies all the angles of his promotions to make sure everything works smoothly, and he really does care about the boxers who appear on his shows. Frank thinks that boxers deserve more dignity and respect than we have been shown in the past, and he goes out of his way to make you feel part of the promotion rather than just a hired hand. Typical of the way he goes about his business is how, on the day that I fought Oliver McCall for the world championship, he sent Laura a huge bunch of flowers on the morning of the fight and had a chauffeur-driven car pick her up to take her to Wembley. That meant a lot to Laura, who says that the Frank Warren office is a joy to deal with in her role as my representative. It all helps a boxer's peace of mind when things run smoothly away from the gym and the ring. It saves Laura giving me a piece of her mind!

When we first got together Frank outlined his exciting plans for me, and he has delivered on everything that he had promised – even down to the Bentley car as a bonus for winning the world championship! I have heard all sorts of whispers and rumours about both Warren and King, but I don't listen to the mischief-makers. I can only go on my experiences with them, and they have both usually come up trumps as far as I am concerned.

It was Frank Warren and Don King who made it possible for Frank to win the world championship at the fourth attempt, but it was Laura Bruno who gave him an even greater prize: their son, Franklin Junior. This was the biggest thrill for the *real* Frank Bruno.

7 : The Real Frank Bruno

'The real Frank Bruno likes to chill out here at home. I go along with all that 'know what I mean' and 'pass the sauce, 'Arry' business in public because it's expected of me. But I switch all that off once I close the gates behind me. '

THERE are two Frank Brunos: the bubbling, buoyant public Bruno, with his 'Know what I mean' catch phrase, booming laughs and 'nice one' greetings for everybody who comes within talking distance; and there's the private Bruno, who likes to hide away from the public gaze and lead a quiet life far removed from the showbiz spotlight and the bedlam of big-time boxing.

You cannot miss the public Bruno because he is such a larger-than-life character. He willingly puts his head above the parapet to become an easy target for the snipers of this world who like to mock his at times torturous clichés and what appears to be a limited vocabulary. But the cynics never get close enough to him to realise that there is much more to him than glib one-liners and the rent-a-laugh genial giant. The private Bruno is an entirely different, and much deeper and more perceptive person than his public persona ever suggests.

There is immediate evidence of how he likes to guard his privacy when you arrive at his Essex mansion home, of which he is rightly proud and protective. This is the house that Frank's fists built, and unsolicited visitors are not encouraged. A spiked fence, an electric security gate and a growl of Rottweilers (Georgina, Bruno and Harriet) are not exactly a welcoming sign. You announce yourself at the entryphone, and Frank, in monogrammed tracksuit, comes bounding down the gravel drive as if on a training run. 'Stay in your car until I get the dogs out of the way,' he says, quite unnecessarily. He shoos them away and then operates the gates with a remote control, and as you drive in and park alongside his Bentley you feel as if you are playing a cameo role in a Hollywood movie. The twisting country lanes leading to the house are hidden behind a boundary of high trees. It's a long, long way from the terraced Wandsworth home in which Frank was living when I first met him some fifteen years earlier.

'Yeah, I have come a long way from Wandsworth,' Frank admits proudly as he gives the grand tour, the dogs loping along behind as if eavesdropping. There are garages with two Mercedes parked, stables with horses contentedly eating their oats, cockatoos, doves and a colourful splash of exotic birds in a huge aviary, two Siamese cats (Delboy and Samson), a newly constructed swimming pool in which Frank powers through thirty lengths a day, a gymnasium packed with boxing equipment, and acres of land that seem to go on for ever. He knows every inch of the land from his daily six-mile run around the sprawling grounds.

Set in the first half of the estate, for an estate is what this is, is the jewel in the Bruno kingdom, an imposing Victorian house that is big enough to demand several entrances. There are two wings, with a further wing having just been added for guest facilities. Inside it is comfortable rather than ostentatious, with a warm, welcoming lived-in feeling. The large kitchen is the hub of the house, with Laura ruling the roost as she prepares lunch for the family: Frank, thirteen-year-old Nicola, nine-year-old Rachel and the now ten-month-old Franklin Junior, who is already looking like a heavyweight in the making. The girls are out riding their horses, Franklin is asleep.

Bruno leads you through a maze of rooms to his tucked-away den, a music room fitted with a DJ's record deck on which he plays loud soul and reggae music. His neighbours, including snooker master Steve Davis, are acres away, so never have cause to complain about the noise. And who would be brave enough to complain, anyway?!

When Frank is relaxed, as now, he drops into impersonating mode, and introduces a range of characters into the conversation. His favourite is the awfully posh Englishman. 'What do you think of the Bentley, old bean? Nice motor, what?' There is also his stereotype West Indian. 'Just lissen to this music, man. Polish your shoes on the dancefloor. *Feel* those vibes, man. Wicked.' When bringing an Irishman into the conversation he mimes as if putting a gumshield into his mouth. 'You tink you're so clever, Bruno, but when the bell goes to start the foight, oi get out of the ring.' He drops easily into Scottish and Welsh accents, and often becomes an American jive-talker. 'Hey, Blood, get your black ass outta here or ah'll come after you with real bad intentions.' And, of course, there is the flash Cockney. 'Leave it out, mate, know wot I mean.' But which is the *real* Frank Bruno?

This is the real Frank Bruno, the one who likes to chill out here at home. I go along with all that 'know what I mean' and 'pass the sauce, 'Arry' business in public because it's expected of me. But I switch all that off once I close the gates behind me. I have never been so contented as I have been since I moved in here. Every morning when I go for my run around the grounds I say a silent prayer of thanks to God for all that I've got. Mind you, I've not been given it on a plate. Everything has had to be earned the hard way. If you don't believe it, try climbing into the ring with a Mike Tyson, a Tim Witherspoon or a Bonecrusher Smith. But it's the only way I could have got where I am today. As well as having to battle it out in the ring, remember I've done my share of slave-labour jobs. I've been a plumber's mate, lugging great baths up winding stairs. I've worked in a beer cellar, had fumes filling my eyes and nostrils while sweating my what's-its off as a metal polisher for twenty-eight quid a week. I've been a builder's labourer carrying a hod of bricks up and down ladders, and I've worked in a bingo hall and as a sports shop assistant. So all this hasn't come easy. Nobody said, 'Here you are, Mr Bruno, here's a bundle of money. Enjoy yourself.' No, mate, I've had to graft for everything I've got, and that's why I appreciate it so much.

It would have been less painful if I could have done it as an accountant, a lawyer or a doctor, but you can only work with the tools that God gives you. My gift was in my fists and I've made the most of it. Boxing has opened doors for me that I could never have dreamed of walking through. I've met all the Royal family, including the Queen, and I'm proud to be an ambassador for the Prince of Wales Trust. I've met Prime Minister Thatcher and Prime Minister Major, and I've chatted to President Clinton at Number Ten Downing Street. I told him that I was going to kick Mike Tyson's ass!

There is hardly a single top entertainer in this country who I have not met or worked with, and I've taken part in the Royal Variety show.

All because of boxing. There is quite a big ham inside the real Frank Bruno, and all that going on stage in pantos and appearing on television with comedians gives me the chance to show off. But I wouldn't give up the day job for it. I know I'm not that good. Boxing's my business and boxing's what has got me where I am. I know that I am repeating myself like a parrot, but all those people who prattle on about banning it should bear in mind that nobody forces me to get in the ring. I do it because I want to and because of the rewards that are there if you are prepared to give every ounce of your concentration to it. I can't stress enough that the money that boxers earn not only improves their lives but also that of their families. I don't think that point is taken into consideration enough when all the ban-boxing debates start.

I can weep buckets for tragic cases like Bradley Stone and James Murray, and for my lovely mate Michael Watson. But they – all of us – know the risks, and are ready to take them for the chance to make a better life for ourselves and for our families. Nobody should be allowed to take that dream away from us. The same way that nobody should stop a man climbing into a racing car, climbing a mountain or doing anything that is considered dangerous. If they want to do it, it should be up to them. Somebody once said to me, 'Better to live like a lion for a day than a mouse for a year', or something along those lines. I understand that. Some people thrive on taking risks. I thrive on boxing, and know all about the dangers.

I consider it important to try to live right so that I am properly prepared for boxing. The so-called bright lights do nothing for me. You can keep your nightclubs and your wild parties that have brought the downfall of many a fine boxing prospect. I think you're just asking for trouble going down that path. I keep right away from it. When I was appearing in panto with Michael Barrymore I remember being in a restaurant late one night when someone came up behind me and made a grab for my black and decker. He was showing off to his mates. That's the nearest I've come to laying out anybody outside the boxing ring. It convinced me that I wanted no part of that late-night so-called swinging scene. I remember another time when I was leaving Wembley after Wimbledon had beaten Liverpool in the 1988 FA Cup Final. A drunken fan started giving me aggravation. 'You're a w-nker, Bruno,' he shouted in a thick Merseyside accent. 'You couldn't knock my old granny over.' He was entiled to his opinion, and I did my best to ignore him as I shuffled along with the crowd filing out of the stadium. For all I knew, his grandmother might have been Supergran.

He wouldn't leave it alone. 'So you're deaf as well, Bruno,' he yelled.

Again I ignored him, and his reaction this time was to charge at me like an angry bull. I sidestepped and the punch that he was aiming at my head glanced off my shoulder. I tensed, ready to hit back in self defence, but thought better of it. 'Leave it out,' I said, as his mates hustled him away. 'It's not my fault Liverpool were beaten.' It was all over in seconds, but it was a lesson to me that I should always be careful.

You have to come here inside my home to find the *real* real Frank Bruno. I'm at my happiest and most relaxed when I'm here with Laura and the kids. Don't know where I'd be without Laura. She's been like a rock to me. Nobody can say she trapped me and married me for my money because when we first met she was earning more than me. I was slaving on a building site, and she was a qualified children's nurse. She's magic with children. Nicola and Rachel couldn't have a better mum, and to see her – and me – with Franklin Junior you would be convinced that we were the proudest parents on earth.

We love Nicky and Rache to bits, and it made everything complete when Franklin was born. It was up there as the greatest day in my life, along with when each of my gorgeous daughters was born. Yes, it was even greater than winning the world title. I was there at the birth, and what Laura went through was ten times tougher than anything I've ever faced in the ring. It was a Caesarean birth, and I was there doing my Steven Spielberg bit with a camcorder because we wanted a record of this great moment in our lives. My hands were shaking so much I could hardly hold the camera, and when little Franklin came out I was crying like a baby. It was magical. Unbelievable. Wicked. And just about every day since Franklin's birth has been special.

All of us, Laura, Nicky and Rache, spend hours just watching him. I know I'm biased, but he really is a fabulous boy. Laura says he's the image of me, even down to the two-line frown on his forehead. But he's much better looking! He seems to be growing by the hour, and shows enormous strength. My mum says I was the same at his age. Always trying to crash my way out of the cot.

I'm often asked if I want Franklin to be a boxer. All I want is for him to be happy. I will encourage him with whatever he wants to do. I'd rather he took up golf or tennis than boxing, but I will not try to make him do anything that he does not want to do. As long as he's happy and healthy. That's all that concerns me.

The same with the girls. Thank God, I can afford for them to get the best possible education to give them a start. Then it's up to them. I won't try to force them into any direction in life. I just want them to grow up very contented and with good common sense and the right attitudes. I want them to be polite and nice people, but not doormats. I want them to have confidence, and to be always surrounded by the love of a close family. That means everything to me. Laura, Nicola, Rachel and Franklin Junior have made the real Frank Bruno a very happy man. A very happy, *family* man.

A visit to the Bruno home is not complete without a peep into his wardrobe, which is a Technicolor salute to the tailoring industry. There are made-to-measure suits of every imaginable shade of blue, along with reds, yellows, greens and pinks. 'With a physique like mine I can hardly keep a low profile,' he says, 'so I might as well wear the sort of bright colours that I like.' Enter the American jive talker: 'Be careful of the threads, dude. They's mah peacock clothes. If you wanna be understood, you've gotta look good.'

There is just time before lunch for Frank to ride his horse, a chestnut hunter called Basil. They are a pair of well-matched heavyweights. With his hard hat on, Frank looks almost boyish and, for such a huge man, he is surprisingly comfortable and lightly balanced as he canters around the Bruno range. 'I learned to ride at Oak Hall,' he reveals. 'But I'm a novice compared to Laura and the girls. They get a lot more out of riding than I do, and that gives me tremendous satisfaction to see them enjoying themselves so much. And it's all down to boxing.'

I must be careful in painting this portrait of the *real* Frank Bruno not to make him sound like Mr Perfect. He would not expect it, and it would not be an accurate portrayal. There is a dark, brooding side to Frank, and if he ever feels he is being taken for granted or that somebody is trying to be too clever by half with him he can become a formidable enemy. He is quick to call on the advice and protection of his lawyer Henri Brandman if he thinks he is being wronged, and many people who have gone to him thinking they are about to deal with 'thick as two short planks' Frank get a nasty shock when they discover that he and Laura are an astute couple who know their value. He has a temper that is buried deep, but when it erupts he can become angry to the point of unreasonableness. The real Frank Bruno does not suffer fools gladly; in fact he does not suffer them at all. He attracts hangers-on because of who and what he is, but he gives them no encouragement and they quickly fade away. When he is getting bad vibes or being pestered beyond the call of celebrity duty he can send a shiver through the strongest of men with a cold-eyed stare that could freeze an eskimo. Don't mess with Bruno when he's in this mood!

But the Frank Bruno that you find chilling out at home with his family is as nice a person as you could wish to meet, and somebody who deserves every break that has come his way. Like Frank says, he has worked for everything he has got. Nobody has given him a thing.

As you make your way back to your car (trying not to look too enviously at the Bentley), Frank brings the Rottweilers under control with a barked command. 'I'm not the greatest dog lover in the world,' he confides, 'but I like having these around because they discourage intruders. There are a lot of nutters out there, and when they see and hear these friends of mine they quickly get the message that they are not welcome.'

Two doves are wooing each other on the back lawn. Frank points them out with that booming belly laugh of his. 'That sums up my life here. Loving and peaceful, know what I mean.'

As I drive off with another chapter in the life and times of Frank Bruno under my belt, I think back to the young man that I first knew as an eighteen-year-old building site worker, who used to try to fiddle his way on to the London underground without a ticket.

Now the *real* Frank Bruno has found his ticket to paradise.

8 : Here's Harry

'All those critics who have said I'm chinny don't know what they're talking about. That punch from Jumbo Cummings would have knocked out most heavyweights, but I managed to come back to win.'

HARRY CARPENTER and Frank Bruno go together like bacon and eggs, Morecambe and Wise and Marks and Spencer. They transcended the usual commentator-sportsman relationship to the point where they were for several years one of the nation's favourite double acts. But on the memorable night when Frank at last became world heavyweight champion, Harry was missing from the Wembley ringside.

Harry had hung up his microphone a year earlier, and he now spends much of his time at his retirement home in the French district of Cognac, where his son, Clive, is an executive with the famous brandy company. Like me, Harry had been urging Frank to retire following his defeat by Lennox Lewis. But there was no happier man in France the night that Frank became champion at the fourth time of asking. 'I watched the fight on satellite television,' said Harry. 'It was an incredible display of sheer determination by Frank. He could hardly hold himself up in that final round but got through it with an unbelievable show of guts. I was thrilled to bits for him. It was a deserved reward for what was almost superhuman perseverance.'

The two were so closely linked that Carpenter even called his autobiography, *Where's Harry?* This was a reference to the night that Frank beat Joe Bugner, a fight screened live from Tottenham's White Hart Lane football ground by ITV. As Jim Rosenthal climbed through the ropes for the after-fight interview, following the demolition of Aussie Joe, Frank looked round and said: 'Where's 'Arry?' For once in his career, Jim was very nearly lost for words.

One of the most exciting moments of Harry's distinguished broadcasting career came when Frank fought Mike Tyson the first time around. Unusually for him, he allowed his bias to come through loud and clear after Frank had staggered Tyson with a sweeping left hook in the first round. 'Get in there, Frank!' Carpenter yelled. Not quite the done thing for a BBC commentator.

'It was probably the most unprofessional thing I ever did at the microphone,' Harry later admitted sheepishly. 'But if Frank could have landed just one more solid punch in those few seconds when Tyson was all over the place he could easily have caused what would have been one of the boxing upsets of the century.'

Harry came temporarily out of retirement to do the interview work on a filmed feature about Frank before the return fight with Tyson. I had the privilege of listening in on their chat on and off camera, and this is a transcript of part of the conversation which captures their special affinity. I include the times that the chat was punctuated with Frank's booming, right-from-the-belly laughter.

HC: First of all, on the bright side, Frank, what would you say is the hardest punch you've ever thrown?

FB: It's one of three, Harry. A left hook, right uppercut against Mike Jameson in my first fight in America was a bit special. The best combination I've ever thrown. Then there was the nuclear right that knocked Gerrie Coetzee through the ropes in a world title eliminator. It landed high on his temple and sent him 'bye 'byes. The referee could have counted to a hundred. D'you remember what you shouted, Harry? I've watched it dozens of times on video, and you sounded like a parrot. 'He's out! Out! Out!' you yelled. Shouldn't get so excited, mate. It's bad for the old blood pressure *(booming laugh)*.

HC: Yes, you did used to make me forget myself at times Frank. It's quite embarrassing to listen to some of those commentaries, but that's the effect you had on me.

FB: And on my opponents *(booming laugh)*. Seriously though, the third hardest punch was against the Cuban José Ribalta. He'd been saying a lot of nasty things about me before the fight. Said he was going to blind me. That was out of order. I put everything into a banana bomb of a right hand, and his lights went out while was he was still standing.

HC: Ribalta nearly finished up in my lap.

FB: Yes, Harry, you needed danger money that night.

HC: Now I've got to pin you down, Frank, to naming just one punch as the hardest you've thrown.

FB: I'd have to choose the right against Coetzee. He'd been a world champion and had beaten some of the best heavyweights around. He'd only been stopped twice before, but I got him out of the way in double quick time. He told me afterwards that nobody had ever hit him as hard in his life. To be honest, I don't think he knew what hit him. It was a punch in a million.

HC: Now a question that you won't be so keen to answer. What is the hardest punch you've ever had to take?

FB: Can't remember, Harry *(booming laugh)*. Actually that's almost the truth. I remember you interviewing me after I had stopped Jumbo Cummings in seven rounds, and you asked me about a punch that landed in the first round and I said, 'What punch was that, Harry?' I did my upright stiff-dummy act after he had crashed an overarm right on my chin. Didn't know whether it was Christmas or Easter, and the bell came to my rescue. All those critics who have said I'm chinny don't know what they're talking about. That punch from Jumbo would have knocked out most heavyweights, but I managed to come back to win. Bonecrusher and Tim Witherspoon also had me in trouble, but they couldn't take me out with one punch.

HC: You must have been devastated by that first defeat by Bonecrusher.

FB: Yes and no. Obviously I didn't enjoy getting beaten and having the granny knocked out of me. But in a way it did me a favour. It was a test of my character. Thank God, I proved I could take a defeat and come back strong. That's when you find out about yourself, Harry.

The glory's easy to live with. It's the defeats that prove what you're really made of. You lost faith in me that night, Harry. Remember? As I went over for the first – and, please God, only – knock out defeat of my career you said, 'This looks like the end of the Frank Bruno story.' But I proved you wrong, didn't I mate?

HC: Yes, I'm delighted to say that you proved everybody wrong. You went on to earn a title fight with Tim Witherspoon, and you were doing wonderfully well against him but then suddenly started running out of steam after about eight rounds.

FB: You're right, Harry. George Francis said I was like a mad motorway driver with his foot down on the accelerator all the time. Eventually I just ran out of gas. It was anybody's fight going into the eleventh round, and I was proud of my performance because I think that history will prove that Tim Witherspoon was one of the better champions. He had a good chin, and that bowled-over right of his was like a sledgehammer landing. He was hitting me with a hammer, Harry, not 'witherspoon'! *(booming laugh)*.

HC: Moving on now, Frank, to your first world title fight against Mike Tyson.

FB: Yes, Harry. I remember it well. Most of all, I remember the cheque!

HC: I've never been so excited at a microphone before.

FB: Tyson was body-popping in the ring, and you were body popping at the microphone.

HC: Why didn't you follow up when you had him staggering with that left hook in the first round?

FB: It wasn't for the want of trying, Harry. I was desperate to give him another one on the whiskers, but he got so close to me it was almost as if he was trying to make love. I just couldn't get him off to get the leverage for another punch. Everybody said that I stood off. I didn't.

He just didn't give me the room to throw another big punch.

HC: Will it be different the next time around?

FB: It's a different Frank Bruno from that first time. I'm bigger by a stone and a half, stronger, more confident, and I'm in a better frame of mind, while I reckon those three years in prison must have taken a lot away from Tyson. Look at his fight with Buster Mathis. I was sitting about four rows back watching the fight and I was in more danger of being hit by some of Tyson's punches than Mathis. I've never seen so many wild misses.

HC: You did better than most people expected against Lennox Lewis.

FB: But not better than I expected, Harry. I expected to win, and I was well on the way to victory until he produced that cracking left hook from nowhere in the seventh round. That was the lowest point of my career. I had pumped myself up into convincing myself that I could and would win. Everything was going to plan, and then wham, bang goodnight ma'am.

HC: Many of us thought you should have hung up your gloves there and then.

FB: I know you had good motives for telling me to pack it in, but I don't think you quite understood what winning a world title meant to me. I know I am sounding like a parrot when I say that I had a dream, but I really did. I was not saying it to sell tickets. I had always seen myself in my mind's eye as champion of the world, with the Belt being buckled around my waist. ' ...and the *new* world heavyweight champion, Frank Brun-o-o-o-o.' When you've got a vision like that, Harry, you've got to see the job through, or become very frustrated.

HC: How do you see your long-term future?

FB: I don't want to look past Mike Tyson at the moment. But when I do decide to hang up my gloves I want to chill out at home and watch my family grow up. Nicola is already a fine young lady, with a good mind on her. Rachel is as bright as a button and full of personality, and Franklin Junior is going to take up a lot of my time. I'll probably do the odd bit of pantomime if they'll have me, and I would like to do some telly work. I enjoy that. I shall also pay more attention to Laura. She's had to put up with a lot because of my commitment to boxing. I owe her so much, not only for being a good wife and mother but because of the brilliant way she handles my affairs away from boxing. The rest of the time I'll be a farmer, with a piece of straw in my mouth and I'll lie back watching the clouds roll by. I'll be able to tell my grandchildren about the days when I fought people like Bonecrusher Smith, Iron Mike Tyson, Terrible Tim Witherspoon and Oliver 'the Atomic Bull' McCall. I just hope they don't get bored listening to me.

HC: Frank, you don't know how to be boring.

FB: That's very nice of you, Harry. I would like to wish you a long a and happy retirement, and enjoy smelling the flowers down in France.

HC: Right, that's a wrap fellers. You can turn the cameras and microphones off now.

FB: Uh, Harry.

HC: Yes, Frank?

FB: I don't know how to tell you this, but your wig has slipped. *(booming laugh)* Know what I mean, Harry!

Harry returned to his retirement in Cognac. Frank went off to the Canary Islands to prepare for his return battle with Mike Tyson. The Frank Bruno show was on the road again.

9 : Tyson Revisited

*'I am a *professional*, and as world heavyweight champion I was entitled to expect the best possible deal...I wanted respect and proper reward as the champion. I did not feel as if I was getting it.'*

A VOLCANIC mountain stood between Frank and his return fight with Mike Tyson. Trainer George Francis turned the holiday island of Tenerife into a punishment zone as he pushed the WBC world champion through a six-week training programme that tested and challenged fitness fanatic Frank as never before. Each day at dawn he was driven by car 2,500 metres up the narrow, twisting paths of Mount Teide where he would run in the rarefied air for forty-five minutes. He would then be forced through an exhausting series of explosive exercises, with Francis bullying him to greater effort that each day brought Frank to his knees. This altitude training was designed to help improve his lung power and stamina.

The uniqueness of this chapter is that it is being written just two weeks before the title fight against Tyson, so all of Frank's recorded thoughts and emotions are spontaneous and not cooked up in retrospect. In all the years that I have been associated with Frank, I have never known him in a more determined nor, at times, angry mood. Let's get the anger out of the way first. For a start, there was aggravation over Frank's pay packet...

When the fight against Tyson was first announced the newspapers were full of talk about this being the one hundred million dollar showdown. 'Great,' I thought. 'As champion I should get the pay deal of a lifetime.' It had been explained to me how Sky were going to use the fight to launch a new television concept called pay-per-view. This meant that their subscribers would have to invest a one-off fee to watch the fight. It was worked out that if just 20% of their five million viewers paid a fee of £10 that would generate an extra £10 million in the UK alone. But once all the ballyhoo had died down I found that the bottom line was that I would be paid £4 million for my first title defence. Now I don't want this to come across as Bruno being 'a bloody greedy, money-grabbing so-and-so'. Boxing is the hardest of all sports. There is enough evidence to show that you put your life on the line when you climb between the ropes. I promise you that I don't do it for fun. I am a *professional*, and as world champion I was entitled to expect the best possible deal. There were all sorts of stories appearing about Tyson, the challenger, getting three times my purse, and that promoter Don King was taking the biggest slice of the cake. The Lennox Lewis camp were trying to stir things up by talking about the bad deal I had done, and that Tyson and King were milking most of the money for themselves. But I ignored what was coming from their direction because I knew they just wanted to get under my skin. To be honest, it did not bother me what they claimed King and Tyson were getting. I am wise enough to know that the name Tyson on the bill was the big attraction. But I wanted respect and proper reward as the champion. I did not feel as if I was getting it.

I tried hard to keep my mind off the money matters because I had wanted to go into the fight against Tyson without the sort of distractions that weighed me down the first time we met. I had been expecting a lot more money than I was paid for the Joe Bugner fight, which was the contest before my challenge for Tyson's title. The joint promoter Barry Hearn had been talking telephone numbers, but the final take was nothing like the newspapers were reporting.

I was determined to be right both physically and mentally for the second fight. Yet I could not help being bugged by the thought that I was not getting the proper payment. This was the earning chance that every boxer dreams about, and I wanted to grab it with both hands. As I say, I was not being greedy but business like. I just wanted what I felt I was entitled to as the defending heavyweight champion of the world.

It all threw something of a cloud over my preparation, but it also made me even more resolved to give the fighting performance of my life against Tyson. But I could have done without the hassle during the build-up to the most important contest of my career.

There was extra aggravation for Frank with the publication of Sunday newspaper allegations that he was risking his life by popping 150 vitamin pills a day. That really got him steamed up, and he came out fighting to knock down the story...

I have always been, and always will be, opposed to drugs. Right through my career I have spoken out against the dangerous habit, whether involving sportsmen or anybody else. My slogan has always been, 'Only mugs touch drugs.' Sadly, drug taking has been part and parcel of the American boxing scene for a long time. I remember meeting the then world champion Larry Holmes on my first visit to the United States when I was a young professional. He took me to one side and said, 'I have just one bit of advice that I want you to listen to, "Don't get involved with coke."' Several of the heavyweights around at the time were getting themselves hooked on the habit, and I appreciated Larry pointing me in the right direction. Not that there was ever any chance of me touching drugs, soft or hard. So you can imagine how angry and upset I was while training in Tenerife to hear that I was being portrayed back home as some sort of junkie. The story said that I took 150 vitamin tablets every day. What rubbish! Why couldn't somebody just have checked this out with me? For a start, where would I get the time to pop 150 tablets every day? The rattling as I went on my training run after taking them would have been heard right across Tenerife!

Yes, I often take a few vitamins with my food but nothing you cannot get across any chemist's counter and just a handful, like millions of other people. The story really hurt me because I go out of my way to tell all the kids I meet that they should stay clear of drugs. I am lucky to have them looking up at me as some sort of role model, and the last thing I wanted was having them think that I am a pill popper. I get most of my vitamins from the good, fresh food that I eat, and my physique is down to hard work in the gym. Drugs play no part in my life.

On top of the aggravation there was also anxiety for Frank in Tenerife when a story broke that ex-WBO champion Tommy Morrison had tested HIV positive. Morrison had been scheduled to fight in Las Vegas, but was refused permission to box following the shock result of his test by a doctor licensed by the Nevada Athletic Commission. A distant relative of Hollywood star John Wayne, Morrison had been a self-confessed playboy who boasted of bedding more than one thousand women.

My first thought was one of sympathy for Tommy, who has now got serious problems. Then I started thinking selfishly, and felt relieved that my fight against Tyson was going to be in Las Vegas where AIDS tests for boxers are compulsory. It's not like that in other countries, and Nevada is only one of five states in America that insists on the test. I am not suggesting that Mike might be HIV, but these days you must take no chances. Ours is a sport in which blood often flows, and there is no knowing what your opponent or his partner has been getting up to or where they have been mixing. The British Boxing Board of Control is, quite rightly, very strict on the matter and the Morrison affair will surely make all countries sit up and realise that they must take the AIDS issue seriously. The South African governing body decided to screen all their boxers in 1995, and no fewer than 34 were found to be carrying the HIV virus. That is really scary, and I will be happier when all boxers are automatically screened before every fight.

Frank usually did his foundation training in Lanzarote, but for the return fight with Tyson he switched to nearby Tenerife on the recommendation of his pal Nigel Benn. He was in the Canary Islands preparing for his WBC super-middleweight title defence against Thulane Malinga, and suggested Frank join him. Benn had become one of the main motivators in Frank's boxing life. 'We're like blood brothers,' said Benn. 'I don't think Frank has been given nearly enough credit and respect for what he has achieved, both for himself and for his country. Too many people look to take the mickey out of him when they're not fit to tie the laces on his boxing boots.'

It was a conversation after Frank's title-winning victory over Oliver McCall that prompted Nigel to persuade him to go to Tenerife. 'Frank told me how knackered he had felt in the fight against McCall,' Benn explained. 'He is one of the fittest people walking this earth, but he has this stamina problem. I told him there was a sure way to fix it.

"What's that?" asked Frank. I said, you've got to take on the challenge of "The Mountain". I knew that would grab Frank's attention 'cos he loves a challenge. He runs half marathons and is always looking for something harder to do in training. I knew The Mountain would sort him out and give him the kind of stamina work that he needed.'

Nigel was right about The Mountain. I went trotting up there thinking that it was going to be a doddle for me because I love running. But the first couple of times I felt as if I had been punched in the solar plexus after running only half the distance that I do at home. I had trained at altitude just once before back in the days when I sparred with a sixteen-year-old kid called Mike Tyson. That was up in the Catskill Mountains, but I didn't do any serious running. I couldn't believe how my breath left me when I started running up the mountain track in Tenerife. George Francis had a wicked grin on his face as he watched me gasping for air. He kept on about the beautiful view as he watched the sun rise, but I was too busy fighting for my breath to appreciate the spectacular surroundings. After two or three days I started to acclimatise, and within a week I was covering the same sort of distances as at home. At the end of each run I was feeling exhilarated, and after a series of muscle-strengthening exercises I would go back for breakfast and then sleep like a baby. Nigel's influence also told at the breakfast table. He had talked me into trying a mixture of boiled chicken and fish, and I can honestly say I have never felt healthier or fitter before a fight.

All the way through I have had George to motivate me and my masseur Rupert to relax me, and Nigel has contacted me most days to give me that extra boost. Like me, he is a great believer in positive thinking and he has kept my mind zeroed in on winning. He keeps talking tactics to me, and telling me that I can blast out any heavyweight in the world provided I follow through with my punches.

Visitors to the Bruno training camp at the smart Royal Sunset Beach Club in Tenerife could not quite believe they were watching the Frank Bruno who had clowned his way into their hearts over the last ten years. This was a new and mean Bruno. He was more serious and intense than I had ever seen him, and he rarely performed any slapstick play acting for the holidaymakers who queued to watch him training for two hours each afternoon. He was wearing his mental blinkers and concentrating purely on getting himself as fit as possible for the fight he had dreamed about ever since Tyson had stopped him in five explosive rounds in Las Vegas in 1989.

Frank had a procession of four large American sparring partners under orders to fight the Tyson way, with clusters of swinging hooks and lots of uppercuts. They took turns to climb into the ring with Bruno, who regularly boxed through twelve rounds with his sparring partners taking three rounds each. There was no question about his fitness, and neither was there any doubt about his intent.

'I've sparred lots of rounds with Frank, and this is the meanest I've known him,' announced Texan Everett "Big Foot" Martin after one particularly punishing session. 'He is really wound up for this fight with Tyson. I think Mike would wish himself back in prison if he could see the way he is shaping up. All of us in the thud and blood business know Mike ain't what he was. Those three years in jail have taken their toll. You can't sit in a cell for three years and then come out and carry on as though nothin' has happened. The biggest mistake Tyson can make is underestimating Frank. He is taking him too soon after two pushovers that proved nothin' to nobody. Frank is a much better fighter than when they last met. His hand speed has improved beyond all recognition, and if there's a heavier hitter out there then I'm glad I've not come across him.'

News came through from an American fight reporter that Tyson had knocked out two of his sparring partners in training and put them in hospital. It would have frightened the life out of most people, but Bruno led the laughter. 'That,' said Big Foot, 'is the oldest publicity stunt in the business. We all know how Mike's been training. His sparring partners are ordered to hold back their punches, and he just belts the daylights out of them. It's like hitting a punchbag.'

Bruno overhears in between his exercises. 'I've got one question to ask you, boy,' he says in an authentic sounding southern States accent. 'If Tyson's in such great shape, why's he training behind closed doors? Well boy? You ain't got an answer, have you? Well I'll tell you what the answer is. He's looking so bad in training that they daren't let the press reporters in to watch him. What's he got to hide, eh boy?'

Bruno then returns to a furious series of exercises. There are ten minutes of high knee-bend skipping, another ten minutes on a rowing machine, a furious session on the heavy punchbag, six minutes of lightning combinations on the punchball and then twenty minutes of throwing punches to order against coaching handpads worn by Francis. This is followed by an exhausting twenty minutes of calisthenics, culminating in Francis dropping a huge medicine ball on to his stomach ten times in rapid succession. It would kill most people, but at the end of it Frank, with black pearls of perspiration bubbling on his face, laughs like a little boy having his tummy tickled. He drops back into the southern accent. 'One of these days, boy, ah'm gonna kick your white ass for dropping that ball on me,' he tells George. 'But first of all I wanna drop some big punches on Mike Tyson's chin. You'd better believe it.'

The gymnasium reverberates to Bruno's booming laugh, and it is so infectious that the holidaymakers join in. It is the first time that they have seen the old Frank come to the surface. The training session is over.

After a dinner of chicken and pasta washed down with pints of pure fruit juice, Frank and George set off on a five mile evening walk. The sun they watched rise over Punishment Mountain is now going down in the west, turning the Atlantic horizon crimson and gold. Somewhere over there Mike Tyson is waiting, and it is to Tyson that their thoughts turn. George quietly goes through all of Tyson's strengths and weaknesses. He has been around in the hit and hurt game too long to even think of trying to lull Frank into a false sense of confidence. But after pointing out all the things that Tyson does well – the left hook, right cross combination, and the lightning uppercut that he likes to bring up from his waist at close-quarters – George starts to reflect on all the things that Frank has got going for him. 'You're bigger and stronger than you've ever been...your hand speed is quicker than Tyson will remember...your improved two-fisted combination punches can do to Tyson just what Buster Douglas did to him...and the extra weight you're carrying from when you first met will help you wear Tyson out in the clinches.'

They walk along the beach at a brisk pace compared to the leisurely tread of the holidaymakers, who are treated to 'Nice one' greetings as they recognise the familiar figure in his Frank Bruno monogrammed tracksuit. Those who get close enough are handed one of the postcard-size autographed photographs of which Frank gives away hundreds during the course of a year.

The man who has been portrayed as a walking cliché by programmes like *Spitting Image* and a score of impressionists becomes almost poetic as he looks out at the sunset. 'Look at that, George,' he says, pointing out to sea. 'How can people say there's no God? What human being could create anything as beautiful as that? I just wish Laura and the kids were here to see it. That's God's paintwork, that is. Makes you feel humble, don't it.'

Back at the training camp, Frank makes one of his frequent telephone calls home to Laura. He catches up on domestic news, talks to Nicola and Rachel and manages to coax a 'Da-da' response from Franklin Junior. He delegates business matters for his lawyer Henri Brandman and then, each in turn, kisses goodnight on the telephone to Laura, Nicola, Rachel and Franklin, who he is told is trying to chew the telephone line at the other end

There is a hint of a tear in Frank's eyes as he replaces the receiver.

This is the hardest moment of the day. When I am in the gymnasium or running up the mountain I give it my full concentration and attention, so nothing is allowed to distract me. But now there is nothing to stop me thinking, and this is when being away from home really hurts. I love my family to bits, and it is the worst punishment of all being away from them. Since I came out here Franklin has started taking his first steps. Missing things like that. God, that is really tough to take.

They are all going to come out for a couple of days before I leave for the United States, but I won't be able to really relax with them until after the fight. I make all this work in my favour. I tell myself that this is all Mike Tyson's fault. He's the man stopping me seeing my family. I make myself really angry thinking about it, and picture myself punching Tyson in the face until he goes down on his back, floundering like a huge black beetle. I remember getting very emotional six years ago before the first Tyson fight when I appeared on a live hook-up

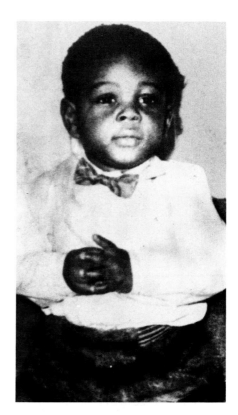

Right: Frank and the young hands of a future heavyweight champion of the world.

Below: A lap of honour for Frank, with his mother, Lynette, father, Robert, and sister Joan.

Frank's father, Robert, who was his main inspiration when he was a young boy growing up in South London. His main advice was, 'Always do what your mother tells you. She knows best.'

Frank (fourth from right) on a day trip to the South Coast with schoolmates from Oak Hall. 'We were a bundle of trouble,' says Frank, 'but school discipline was so strict that few of us stepped too far out of line.'

Happy families. Frank and Laura (above) with their daughters Nicola and Rachel; and Frank (right) with his maternal grandmother Henrietta Brown from Jamaica.

Frank is happily brought to his knees by the lights of his life, his daughters Nicola and Rachel. The Bruno family was completed in 1995 by the arrival of Franklin Junior

This is Frank in the earky years of his career at the age of twenty, and managing to look older than he does now in his mid-thirties! 'That moustache put years on me,' says Frank.

A left uppercut shakes Peter Mulendwa (above) and a right uppercut finishes off Mike Jameson (below) in what was Frank's American debut.

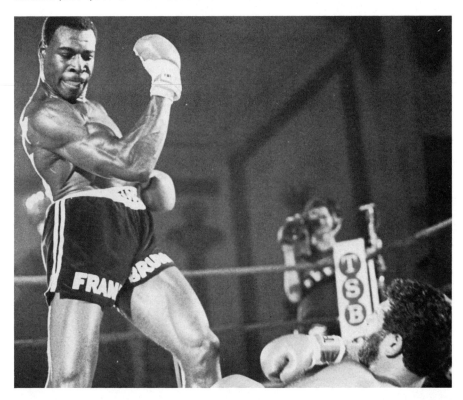

Above: A left cross staggers Winston Allen just moments before the referee came to his rescue in round two.

Left: It's the road leading to the first Mike Tyson fight. Trainer George Francis accompanies Frank at the start of a six mile early-morning run.

Right: The home gym, with Frank getting some training tips from daughter Rachel.

Below: The home trophy room in which Frank keeps his hard-earned prizes. This picture was taken before he collected the world championship belt.

from America with Terry Wogan's studio in London. Without telling me, they had Nicola and Rachel in the studio. I recall that when Rachel saw me waving to her she went and kissed the screen. That really cut me up, and I had tears rolling down my cheeks. Some people saw it as a sign of weakness, but I see nothing wrong in showing your emotions where your family is concerned.

I hate being away, but the way I look at it is that I am like a soldier away at war. Once the battle is over I can go home, but until then I must stay on red alert because there are going to be a lot of bombs dropping ... mostly, I hope, on Mr Tyson's chin.

Not being able to see my family stokes up my appetite for the fight. I am really hungry for Tyson. He is going to taste my punches. The nearer the fight comes the more hungry I get, the meaner I become and the blacker my moods. This is the other Frank Bruno. As George said when he took over as my trainer, 'No more Mr Nice Guy.'

Rupert Doaries – 'Mr Magic Hands' to Frank – arrives to give one of his regular full-body massages. Frank rarely lets a day go by without a massage, even when he is not preparing for a fight. He likes to keep his huge muscles loose and is as carefully handled as a thoroughbred racehorse.

Poker-faced Rupert is the butt of a lot of Bruno jokes, but just gets on with his job of kneading heavily oiled muscles so that the pain of the day's hard toil is quickly forgotten. Rupert was once very close to Lennox Lewis, yet here he is happily installed in the 'enemy' camp. Daily reports reach the Bruno camp that Lennox and his advisers are still battling through American courts to try to get the title defence against Tyson called off. Don King and Frank Warren have assured Frank that the fight will go ahead, and he pushes the fight-off scare stories out of his mind.

I am well prepared for anything the Americans throw at me. Look at the way they messed me around before my first fight with Tyson. It was originally due to take place at Wembley Stadium in June 1988. It was finally staged eight months later in Las Vegas after seven other dates had been pencilled in and then rubbed out. When I reported to the Las Vegas hotel where I was staying in the final two weeks they treated me like a piece of dirt. When I complained the hotel publicist put out a story that 'the Englishman appears to have been affected by the pressure surrounding the fight.' This time I'm going to be ready for them. I want to be treated with the respect that a champion deserves. The Yanks don't like the world heavyweight title – any version of it – being outside the United States, and they will be doing their best to needle me and upset my concentration. But they will be wasting their energy. I am completely focused on the fight.

Frank is drifting off under Rupert's rhythmic hand movement, and when the 30-minute massage is finished he showers and then retires to bed. It is 9pm. He is sound asleep within minutes of his head hitting the pillow. It will be five o'clock the next morning when the alarm bell will ring to signal that Punishment Mountain is again waiting to challenge him. Because it's there.

As Frank goes to sleep, a disc jockey at a beachside disco a mile away slips on the latest soul record. It is Nigel Benn at the turntable, relaxing after his punishing day of training. 'Frank and I are different animals,' he says. 'We are both fitness fanatics, but we go our own ways when it comes to switching off. Frank likes to get his head down, while I like to go out and enjoy myself. Frank is training at different times to me because he wants his body clock to be on Las Vegas time, while I will be fighting in Newcastle.'

Asked about Bruno's chances against Tyson, Nigel is as positive with his views as he is with his fighting. 'If he fights the way I've been telling him, he will win,' he says. 'The Americans are really worried about this one, believe me. I will be at his side in Las Vegas and making sure nobody takes any liberties with him. I've been there, done that. Doug DeWitt and Iran Barkley were both going to tear me apart when I went over there, but I beat them both. So I've proved I know how to overcome the obstacles they put in your way when you are a foreign fighter in the States.'

He turns the record over, and then continues on his 'I'm-backing-Bruno' theme. 'They'll try all sorts of tricks to try to unsettle and aggravate Frank, things like mislaying the key to the gymnasium and calling press conferences at the most inconvenient time. I've stressed to Frank that he has got to act the part of the champion. He should dictate to them, not the other way around. If Tyson turns up at a press conference, then Frank should be there. If Tyson decides he can't be bothered, then Frank should not show his face either. If the weigh-in is staged when it doesn't suit Frank, then he must tell them to change it.'

Benn, who always wears his lion-size heart for all to see, has advised Frank to fight the simple way. 'It's got to be that cracking left jab of Frank's followed by a right hand that can knock anybody's block off,' he said. 'This is Frank's Golden Shot. And I will be there to cheer him on to victory.'

Frank's tactics for the Tyson return were polished and perfected in secret sessions with George Francis. Together they studied the first fight frame by frame. It was noted how it was Frank's left hook that nearly floored Tyson in the first round, and it was also underlined that Frank should not back off to the ropes and so make himself a standing target for Tyson's combinations. They also had a close look at the way Buster Douglas knocked out Tyson in his one defeat. A big pointer was the way Douglas claimed the centre of the ring and kept ramming his left jab through Tyson's guard.

This is Frank talking about his 'Tyson exterminator' plans during the final build up to the showdown in Vegas...

My plan is pretty basic. I'm going to go out from the first bell with the idea of blasting Tyson out of the ring. Too often I've gone into a big fight with the thought of conserving my energy and strength in case it went the distance. But with Tyson, I'm looking for a quick finish – with him on the deck, not me. I am going to try to stop him inside five rounds.

The big mistake I made against him in our first fight was that I was too stiff and upright, and an easy target for those uppercuts of his. Well he won't find my chin so easily this time. I've really worked hard on improving my defence, and Tyson is not going to find me nearly as easy to hit as the last time.

I know in my heart that I am a better and stronger fighter than I was when I first fought Tyson. I was not in a 100 per cent right frame of mind. This time it's different. I'm really up for it, and I just hope

Mike Tyson means it when he says that he thinks it's going to be easy to beat me. He is in for one helluva shock if he truly believes that I am going to be a pushover.

There is no doubt in my mind that those three years in prison have knocked the edge off Tyson. Nobody can tell me that he is even nearly as good as he was when we fought six years ago. People forget that he was already showing signs of losing his power before he was locked away. I was the first to show he was ready to be taken when I rocked him with a left hook in the first round of our 1989 fight. Until then, everybody had claimed that he was indestructible.

Tyson will not be let off the hook this time. It won't be a one-punch finish. I will be looking for nuclear combinations rather than a single shot. If I can stagger him with a left hook, just think what I could do to him with my favourite right.

Buster Douglas saw me give Tyson a fright, and he suddenly knew he was not the great monster that everybody was making him out to be. Tyson has got two legs, two arms and a head that can be hit just like you and me. Douglas knocked the granny out of him before finally putting him down and out in the tenth round. There was that pathetic attempt to get the championship taken off Douglas because the Tyson camp complained that he had failed to beat the count in the eighth round, but every neutral person who saw the fight knew that Douglas had won fair and square.

After losing the title Tyson had two wars with Razor Ruddock when he looked a shadow of his old self. Lennox Lewis got rid of Ruddock in two rounds, which showed he was hardly a world beater, yet Tyson really struggled to beat him. Then it was off to prison, and that's no place for anybody to prepare themselves for boxing.

I have made a close study of both Tyson's fights since his comeback, and I have seen nothing to change my view that he is not the old ferocious force. At his peak, I would say Tyson was one of the all-time greats, up there with Dempsey, Louis, Marciano and Ali. But he is now way past his best. His first comeback fight against Pete McNeeley was a farce – 90 seconds of nothing. If they had put McNeeley in with me there would have been the same sort of uproar that followed my fight against Chuck Gardner. He should not have been in the same arena let alone the same ring as Tyson. It was a joke. You could see that Tyson was embarrassed by it all. He was out of the ring before the official result was announced. Tyson just took his money and ran.

There is no way he will have that sort of easy ride against me. Not in a million years.

Fight number two against Buster Mathis wasn't much better. I sat at the ringside, and I was in greater danger of getting hit by some of Tyson's punches than Mathis. It wasn't as if Mathis was the most mobile or smallest of targets, yet Tyson was missing by miles. It was a sure sign that the three years in prison has robbed him of much of his timing and rhythm, which was so important to him when he was knocking over all-comers. The one word they always used to describe Tyson was awesome. Against Mathis he was awful.

He has made the mistake of his life by taking me too early. I reckon he needed at least another three fights to shake off the ring rust before daring to climb into the ring with me. I would have backed the Bruno of 1989 to beat the present Tyson. Well, the Bruno of 1996 is a much better equipped and stronger fighter and I am convinced I will do the business.

There always used to be a fear factor in Tyson fights. Many of his opponents have frozen before a punch has been thrown. But Mike knows I am not in the slightest bit intimidated or overawed by him. I fought him when he was still terrorising the world's heavyweights and gave him plenty of trouble before he overpowered me.

Since then he has lost a lot of his power, while I have gained weight and increased my punching strength. There are two different fighters climbing into the ring from the last time we met. One is over the hill, and the other one – me – is on top of the mountain. I am a new man since winning the championship. It has done wonders for my confidence and self-belief, and I am determined to return home still in possession of my WBC world championship belt.

I've noticed that Tyson is talking a good fight in interviews in the States, but the old Mike did all his talking in the ring with his fists. When I met him for the announcement of our fight after he had beaten Mathis he was surrounded by menacing looking bodyguards wearing black trilby hats. I know they were trying to frighten the life out of me, but I found them funny rather than frightening. They were chanting and making Ku-Klux Klan lynching gestures at me. I found that part of the pantomime really sickening, and it just made me all the more determined to beat the hell out of Tyson.

They won't be climbing into the ring with Tyson. He'll be all on his own when the bell goes. There'll be just him, me and the referee. Then we'll find out whether he can still do the business. I *know* that I can.

I just hope the referee lets me fight. The last time I was being warned from the first minute for the sort of things that American heavyweights have been doing to Brits for years. If you don't believe me, have a look at old film of Rocky Marciano beating former British champion Don Cockell back in 1955. Marciano hit him with just about everything but the corner stool and fouled him time and again without a murmur from the referee. Tyson has also been known to hit after the bell and to land illegally. I won't mind the referee telling me off provided he treats us both on equal terms.

Tyson's two fights since leaving prison were not even as good for him as gymnasium sparring sessions. I know that deep down he must have doubts about whether he's still got it. Sitting in a prison cell for three years can eat away at your confidence. Nobody can convince me that the Tyson who came out of prison is the same force to be reckoned with as the one who was locked away. He is living on his reputation, and I mean to rip it to shreds.

I have never been so fired up for a fight. All those hangers-on surrounding Tyson really got me wound up. I was told he had done away with all those bad influences, but there they are sucking up to him and telling him all the things he wants to hear rather than what he should be told.

I've not got a personal grudge against Mike Tyson. When we've been together away from the fight business I have always found him a pleasant man, surprisingly quietly spoken and without any arrogance. But he changes once the vultures are at his side, and he came with all that I'm-going-to-stare-you-out rubbish when we posed for the photographers after the Mathis fight. I refused to let his gaze go, and I think he got the message loud and clear that he cannot frighten me. The days when he put the fear of God into opponents just by looking at them have long gone. Now, as far as I'm concerned, he's just another fighter, and I will be treating him with the same respect as I treat any opponent.

What I am fighting for against Tyson is not only revenge for my defeat six years ago but also respect. I want the respect of Tyson, and I want the respect of people who have not given me any credit for winning the world title after so many of them had written me off as finished after Lennox Lewis stopped me.

I'm a changed man since I won the title. Being introduced as *world heavyweight champion* is just about the sweetest thing I've heard. And I want to keep on hearing it. It has done wonders for my pride, and I feel that I have matured both as a person and as a fighter.

There are, I hear, thousands of fans paying to fly to Las Vegas to cheer me on. I could have nearly as many supporters out there as Tyson. That is going to be an extra spur because I will not be wanting to let them down.

I refuse to have a single negative thought about the fight. Paul McKenna got me into a positive-thinking mood before the championship fight against Oliver McCall, and I have carried on from there. In my mind's eye I only see myself winning the fight. I keep hearing about what Tyson is doing to his sparring partners in training, but that goes in one ear and out the other. It's not what you do in the gym that matters but in the ring. Going by Tyson's two performances since his release from prison, I reckon he has gone back about forty per cent, while I think I have improved forty per cent since we last fought.

All my training at altitude has made me feel stronger and sharper than ever, and I just can't wait to get into the ring and to hear the MC announcing, '...and introducing to you, the heavyweight champion of the world, Frank Brun-o-o-o.' Then I want the first bell to ring, so that I can get at Mike Tyson. I've waited six long years for this chance to put the record straight. All I know is that I would not like to be in Tyson's boots when I am coming at him. This time, *I'm* the one with bad intentions.

I like to get a picture of my fights in my mind, and I have this lovely view of Tyson going down to a thumping left right combination to the jaw. He falls through the middle rope right into the lap of promoter Don King, and I stand there with my hands held high in triumph as the referee shouts the 'eight-nine-ten-out' count over the top rope.

Then the American MC almost chokes on his words when he has to announce, '...the winner and *still* heavyweight champion of the world, Frank Brun-o-o-o.'

This was Frank Bruno talking *before* the fight. Now let's move on to the real thing and to the Showdown in Las Vegas...

10 : Showdown in Vegas

'Tyson beat me fair and square. No arguments. No disputes. I wish I had the power to switch off the night of 16 March 1996 and start all over again. I did not do myself justice, and I feel so sorry for all those supporters that I let down.'

Frank *talked* a good fight in the build-up to the showdown in Las Vegas, but he was not allowed to provide action to go with his words by a Mike Tyson who was back to his awesome best. Britain's heavyweight hero climbed into the ring at the MGM Grand Arena a proud champion, and left it a bruised and bitterly disappointed ex-champion who had been comprehensively beaten inside three rounds.

We have endeavoured to make this an honest book about Bruno, and Frank would not want me to duck telling the truth about what happened in his return fight with Tyson, even though the truth hurts. The plain fact is that Frank failed to function in anything like the way he had planned, and he was given a good hiding by a mighty fighter throwing possibly the fastest fists in heavyweight history.

I am not going to use this book to make excuses. Tyson beat me fair and square. No arguments. No disputes. I just wish I had the power to switch off the night of 16 March 1996 and start it all over again. I know that I did not do myself justice, and I feel desperately sorry for all those supporters that I let down. Thousands of them had paid hard-earned money to give me their support in Vegas, and many many more lost sleep time to watch and listen to my fight at home. I wanted so badly to give them something to remember.

Perhaps I wanted it *too* badly. Perhaps I wound myself up so much that I was not loose enough on the night of the fight. I just cannot give honest answers to why it went so badly wrong, but one thing I can say is that Mike Tyson surprised me by his performance. I definitely misjudged him.

I can now say pretty positively that the three years he spent in prison did not diminish his power and certainly not his speed. His hands were even faster than in our first fight back in 1989, and if there have been faster fists in the heavyweight boxing ring then I haven't seen them.

I had got myself into truly believing that I could beat Tyson, and beat him convincingly. My game plan was to claim the centre of the ring and let him run on to my left jab, and then crack him with my right at every opportunity. I had got myself into superb condition after nine weeks of non-stop training. In hindsight, people have said that I was too heavy, but I was convinced that my added bulk from when we first met would help me be like a wall of armour.

My trainer George Francis and I agreed that I should box him, not fight him, and then throw the nuclear punches when I had made the openings. But Tyson did not give me a chance to settle and get my punches off. He was all over me like a harbour shark, and from the first minute I knew that, despite all the rumours, he had got himself into tip-top shape. We had heard that he had been struggling in training and that he was sluggish and uninterested. I just wish *that* Tyson had turned up in the ring!

He was razor-sharp, and quickly got his combination punches working. At times he was almost sprinting towards me to avoid my jab, and was then crashing short hooking punches in from close range. He fought the perfect fight, while I hardly got started on what I intended to do. It was the most frustrating night of my life.

Now that I've had time to reflect on the fight, I still can't say just where I went wrong. I honestly think the answer lies in what Tyson did right rather than what I did wrong. He was punch-perfect from the first bell, while I struggled to get my timing right and was not in command like I had intended. There was so much that I wanted to do but Tyson just did not give me the chance. He was coming at me like an angry bull, and every one of his punches was thrown with bad intentions.

Man, I really had to be on red alert in there, otherwise I could easily have been beaten in the first round. He caught me with a couple of cracking punches, but I held on and tried not to let him know that he had hurt me. I got home with one good right, and a left hook made him grunt but it was nothing like the punch with which I shook him in our first fight.

Near the end of the first round I took a sickening thump to the side of the head and I felt blood trickling from my left eye. On the video replays it looked as if it was caused by a right-hand punch, but I was not sure. Tyson had been reckless with his head and the occasional elbow, while I joined in the jungle warfare by holding and hitting. This was not a kids' party. This was for real, and my precious world championship belt was at stake.

I had not, thank God, had too many cuts during my career, and I have to admit that the sense of blood coming down the side of my face did not help my confidence. I was not in good shape as I returned to the corner at the end of the first round, and I knew in my heart that Tyson had had much the best of it.

All George Francis's concentration in the one-minute interval was on trying to close the gash high on my left eyebrow, and he and my brother Michael just had time to remind me that I needed to be first with my jab. Believe me, I knew that. But to be first against a man as quick as Tyson is much easier said than done. He rocked me with a left-right combination early in the second round, and I had to hang on for my life.

Referee Mills Lane, who had given me a talking to in the first round while ignoring some gutter stuff from Tyson, took a point away from me for holding. I was not too concerned, but what did annoy me was that the referee did not warn Tyson for using his head and elbow. But you know what I always say: *that's cricket!* I planted my feet and got in a couple of solid shots of my own, and I had the satisfaction of landing with a good right uppercut which was the punch I had planned to use as a surprise for Tyson. But I have to concede that the really wicked punches were coming from Tyson and I was forced to give ground.

As his bombardment continued, I tried to put him out of his stride by switching to southpaw as I had in the later stages of my fight against Oliver McCall. It was a waste of time because Tyson just kept bulling his way forward, determined to sweep me out of his path. It was an awesome performance, and if I had been watching at the ringside as a spectator I would have applauded the sheer speed and power of the man. But as I was on the receiving end against this human bulldozer, I was not exactly enjoying the experience.

I promise this is not an excuse, but I was very aware of my eye injury and this was causing me increasing concern as rights from Tyson thumped on to the wound. I tried to push him off and make room to get leverage for my punches, but he was making full use of his shorter reach by bombing away from close range. When I went back to my corner at the end of the second round, I realised I was in for a hot old night. Believe me, Tyson was making it tough in there.

Viewers watching at home were shocked by the language George Francis used when I sat down on the stool. This was the industrial language of the fight game, and I was disappointed that the television microphones were able to pick it up. George pulled no punches as he told me that I was fighting at too slow a pace and needed to speed up. He wanted me to do all the things we had planned over the previous nine weeks, but I could have done with him going over to Tyson's corner to tell him to slow down while I got my act together!

I bit hard on my gumshield and went out for the third round determined to try to stamp my authority on the fight. My aim was to try to keep Tyson at long range because it was when he was getting in close that he was catching me with his hooking punches. I landed what I thought was a good right, but he immediately responded with a clubbing left hook that forced me on the back foot. Then he came charging forward on the sort of two-fisted attack that had first established him as the heavyweight king back in the 1980s. I was too busy defending myself to try to throw any counter punches, and as he drove me back towards the ropes his fists were pumping away in a blur of action.

I was trying too desperately to block them to count them, but the people at the ringside later reckoned they counted ten or eleven that landed in a blinking of an eye. It was an incredible bombing attack. Believe me, I know because I was on the receiving end.

Two uppercuts completely unhinged me, and my left leg came up off the canvas as my nerve ends reacted to the phenomenal power of the punches. I felt as if the sky was falling in as I was half punched and half fell down on to the bottom rope. This was the position in which I had dreamed of having Tyson. Now it was my nightmare.

I was conscious as Mills Lane put his arms around me, shouting, 'That's enough…It's over.' If he had counted, I would have forced myself to get up but there is no question I could then have been in serious trouble because Tyson was waiting with very bad intentions.

So I suppose I have to thank Mills Lane for stopping it when he did. There are other referees who would have taken up a count, and allowed the fight to go on. But I have to say that the referee was right to stop it. Mike Tyson had proved his right to have the WBC championship back. I could not argue with that.

I was in control of myself when I was led back to my corner, and Laura was quickly at my side. At the same time, Tyson came over and said in my ear that he loved me, that he was grateful for the chance to get his title back, and that he wished me luck and God bless. This was the compassionate Tyson I have got to know and like away from boxing. I had the odd experience of having Laura kissing me on the right cheek, while Tyson was kissing my left cheek. All I knew was that I was choked that I had not been able to land a knock-out blow on his kisser, know what I mean! But on the night the man had simply been too good, too quick and too powerful for me.

Despite the hammering I had taken I was well enough to give fairly instant interviews for the American television company. Showtime, and then for Sky Television. It is very difficult to get your thoughts together in moments like that, particularly as it was so soon after I had lost the belt I had promised to take back home to Britain.

I did my best to give a proper assessment of the fight, and kept saying parrot-fashion that Tyson had won fair and square and that, at the end of the day, I had done my best and had no excuses.

But in my heart I knew I had not done my best. I had not produced the form I knew I was capable of, and it will always be a mystery to me why I did not do a better job. But that is not to take a thing away from Tyson. I have stated earlier in this book that at his peak he was up there with the all-time greats like Louis, Ali, Dempsey and Marciano. Well, against me he had proved that he was back to that sort of status, and I know I do not need to feel any sort of shame for losing to such an outstanding fighter.

I think he is good enough to take out any of the current champions, and it is clear that while in prison he obviously took a good look at himself and decided to get himself and his life together. Before he was locked away he was on the downhill slide and there were reports of him drinking heavily, and he was making more headlines with his private and personal life than his boxing.

I am not so sure about some of the people Tyson has around him. Some disgraceful things were said to me and behind my back by people in his entourage, leading up to the fight. If I were Mike Tyson I would ditch them because they give him – and boxing – a bad name.

What broke my heart was the sight of all the disappointed British fans in Las Vegas who had obviously pinned their hopes on me winning, and who had done so much to help me fly the flag for our great country. I wanted to make their trip worthwhile, and it really gutted me that I did not do more to earn their incredible reception.

Mike Tyson must have thought he was fighting in London rather than in Las Vegas, and I apologise from the bottom of my heart that I did not live up to their expectations. I honestly believed that I was going to return home with my belt, but that man Mike Tyson had other ideas. Sorry.

Nigel Benn, who had suffered similar heartbreak when losing his world title two weeks earlier, did his best to put the heart back into his giant pal in the morgue of a dressing-room after the fight. He had led Bruno into the ring, proudly carrying aloft the Union Jack, just as he had when Frank fought Oliver McCall. This time it took a special kind of effort from Nigel, who had disappeared from public view after having his championship ripped from him on an emotional night in Newcastle. He had announced his retirement immediately after the fight and then proposed marriage to his girlfriend by going down on one knee in the centre of the ring.

While Frank was making apologies all round for his performance and cuddling his daughters Nicola and Rachel in a daddy-protective way, Nigel told him: 'Nobody has let anybody down. All those people who came here from Britain to cheer you on don't feel let down. They are just feeling like you – disappointed, that's all.'

Still obviously feeling his own disappointment at losing his title, Nigel added: "If you're looking for somebody who let people down, then take me. I blew it in Newcastle. That was shattering. But I didn't die. I only lost a fight. And that's the same with you tonight. You've only lost a fight, that's all. You did what you had to do. It just happened that on this night the other guy did his job better. Believe me, Frank, everybody's proud of you. You met Tyson on one of his better nights.'

The media were pressing Frank for a statement on his future. 'Everybody will be telling you to retire, Frank,' said Benn. 'I know, because the same has happened to me. But it's up to you, nobody else. We're the guys who know how much we've got left in our tank. Only the fighter knows in his heart when it is time to quit. Don't be rushed, Frank. You decide in your own time, but just remember – you have done yourself, your country and your fans proud.'

Once all the hitting and the hurting was over in Las Vegas, Frank returned home to Essex for specialist medical treatment on the gash over his eye and Mike Tyson started to plan his career as the re-crowned champion. His vowed intent is to unify the title, and few who saw his demolition of Bruno doubt his ability to win all four versions of the world heavyweight championship.

Asked for his view of Bruno, Tyson said: 'Frank is a great guy who I respect as a man both inside and outside the ring. I wish him luck with whatever he plans to do in the future, and I send him and his family my love. We tried to hurt each other there in the ring, but that's our business. It's what we do, and I have this viciousness, this ferociousness inside me that convinces me I can beat any man who gets in the ring against me. That's just the way I am. I was pleased with my performance against Frank, but I still think there is room for improvement. He came into the ring so big, so massive that I knew he would be difficult to miss. I look on Frank as a friend, and I thank him for giving me the opportunity to regain one of my titles. Now I want to unify the championship, and I am ready to fight whoever Don King puts in the ring. It would be nice to unify the titles. That is my objective. This is the first step.'

Frank had not been ex-heavyweight champion of the world more than five minutes before the inevitable conjecture started about his future and whether he should hang up his gloves.

It is at times like this that you have to stand up and be counted, and I had no doubts about advising Frank to retire from the ring for good. The last thing I ever want to see him do is going down the Joe Bugner road of making more comebacks than Frank Sinatra and having to face the indignity of defeat against a relative novice at the age of forty-six.

I am sure Bruno will never need to get involved in this sort of sad scenario. He has earned a lot of money with his fists since turning professional. But, of course, so did Bugner. I know that Frank's money is safe and wisely invested.

He has a wife, Laura, and family who love him to bits, and he returns this love with a fierce passion. I had no doubt that the time was right for him to stop and smell the flowers on his stunning Essex estate, and to watch his two beautiful daughters and his son, Franklin Junior, grow.

Boxing has been good to Bruno. And Bruno has been good to boxing with his dignified approach that has won him a place in the hearts of people who have only a passing interest in the hit and hurt business.

The great majority of people who have Frank's true interests at heart made it clear that they would rather he bow out knowing that the curtain had been dropped on his career by one of the finest and most ferocious heavyweights of all time. But Frank was determined not to be stampeded into a retirement decision, and the Tyson defeat was barely 48 hours behind him before he was exercising his mind about the possibility of another challenge for the world championship.

Everybody but everybody has an opinion on our heavyweight hero and this is a cross-section of the views collected from witnesses of his painful defeat in Las Vegas:

MILLS LANE: 'I had no hesitation in stopping the fight. I looked into Frank's eyes and they were not focused properly. It had not been a dirty fight, but I had to work hard in there to keep them apart. Tyson did his job well and I saw it as my duty to end it there and then. There was no point in letting it go on.'

GEORGE FRANCIS: 'We had planned for Frank to box Tyson, and to try to meet him with a strong left jab. But he was too small and elusive a target. He was coming in much faster than anybody expected, even faster than the old Tyson. He was getting under Frank's reach and banging away with both hands. The cut that Frank got in the first round didn't help matters, but like Frank says, that is not an excuse. On the night we have to admit that the better man won. But it was not for the want of trying by Frank. He was in the best shape of his life, but he just wasn't allowed to fight the way he wanted to. Let's take nothing away from Tyson. He was in terrific form.'

BARRY MCGUIGAN: 'This defeat is terribly sad for Frank and all his fans. He's got nowhere else to go now. He should retire. He's done himself and Britain proud. But now is the right time to retire. We all got caught up in the pre-fight hype and started to believe that Frank could do it. But now that we have seen the fight we have to ask ourselves how we dared to question the ability and the greatness of Tyson. He is just as awesome as he was seven years ago. There was a school of thought that Frank's weight advantage of nearly two stone would make him that much stronger than Tyson. What it did in actual fact was make him that much slower, and Tyson's speed as much as his power was the decisive factor.'

DUKE MCKENZIE: 'At least Frank went out on his shield like a true champion. It would have been easy for him to lay down early on from any of those big punches which Tyson was landing. But he held on, dug in and tried his best to stop the mighty machine coming at him. Frank obviously went into the fight with a game plan, but Tyson was so dominant that the plan went out of the window in the first round. Getting cut and then losing a point for holding did nothing to help his confidence, and the way Tyson finished the fight was just awesome. It looked as if the time out of the ring has done Tyson more good than harm. He was if anything even better than he was before being sent to prison. He has done a lot of growing up, and his new Muslim faith seems to have strengthened him as a person. On the evidence of that performance against Frank, I can't see a heavyweight around to stop him unifying the title.'

SIR JIMMY SAVILE: 'Frank can feel proud of all that he has achieved from humble beginnings. He may have lost the title but he has won life's fight. At more than £1 million per round, he has set up the family he loves so much for life. I suggest he now takes a four-year holiday.'

JOHN CONTEH: 'Tyson's a natural fighter and Frank is not. It's as simple as that. Frank doesn't have that natural instinct…the killer instinct. I thought he should have retired after the Lennox Lewis defeat, but he proved me wrong. It was incredible that he managed to win the world title, and he should now hang up his gloves with that as a proud achievement.'

JOHN MORRIS, BRITISH BOXING BOARD OF CONTROL SECRETARY: 'Frank has to make his own decision about his future, but he can hold his head up high. He did us proud and has no reason to feel that he has let anyone down.'

HARRY CARPENTER: 'If I could have reached into the television screen and hauled Frank out of that ring, believe me, I would have done it. Tyson's hands were as fast and explosive as ever, and I knew from the first minute that it was going to be a night of disaster for our hero. Nobody except Frank could have been more relieved than me when referee Mills Lane stopped it. This was Frank's worst night in all his years as a professional. Now I hope that he goes safely and happily through the rest of his life and leaves the fighting to others.'

Laura Bruno, Frank's wife, soulmate and minder, felt the pain of defeat as deeply as her husband. She sat at the ringside with daughters Nicola and Rachel, who was seeing her daddy box for the first time. Within moments of him returning to his corner at the end of the fight, Laura had raced up the ring steps and was ducking inside the ropes to kiss and console him. 'I just wanted him to know that he had done us proud, and that I loved him so much.'

It was Laura who comforted Frank on the flight home to London and still with the world championship belt. 'That belt had meant so much to Frank,' Laura said. 'It represented all that he had worked for from the first day that he turned professional. It is rightfully his because he earned it with his blood, sweat and tears. I picked up the belt while I was in the ring after the fight, and took it back to the dressing room. Tyson is the new champion, but they can't take that belt away from Frank.'

Laura knows Frank better than anybody, possibly better than he knows himself. She knew just how much he was hurting after his defeat. 'It wasn't a physical pain,' she said. 'The cut over the eye and the bruises will heal. It's the pain he feels deep down inside that won't go away. He believes he has let everybody down, his fans, his family, the whole country. But I have told him he is *still* the champ.'

The most moving moment for Laura came in the dressing-room after the fight. 'I had managed to control my tears until I saw Frank and Nigel Benn together,' she said. 'Nigel was consoling Frank, and it suddenly dawned on me that they were now both ex-world champions. It was really moving to see Nigel trying to cheer Frank up, and I just couldn't stop the tears coming.'

But once the tears had been wiped away, it was time to get priorities right. And for Frank, priority number one has always been the family.

The greatest sacrifice I have made for boxing is not seeing my wife and kids as much as I would like. Once the fight against Tyson was over I could not wait to cuddle Laura, and my smashing girls Nicola and Rachel. I was particularly concerned about Rachel because she is only nine and this was the first time we had allowed her to see me box. She was worried about me because there had been some blood flowing, but I quickly assured her that I was all right.

The greatest moment for me was when I arrived back home with Laura and the girls to be greeted by Franklin Junior. He was full of life and energy, running around whereas when I last saw him at home he had only just about mastered walking. This is when it dawned on me what my life is really about. It is not about boxing and world championships. That has all been a means to an end. My life is about my family and my home. I had been away from them for nearly ten weeks, and it felt more like ten months.

The daffodils were sprouting in the grounds of my beautiful home and everything in the garden was lovely.

As I came through the terminal at the airport after landing in lovely old England I was given a warm welcome by everybody who spotted me, and that made me feel extra good. I had been worrying that I had let everybody down, but just about everyone I speak to tells me that they understood that on the night I was beaten by a better man and that there was nothing to be ashamed about.

Now that I have had time to think about the fight, I realise that I met a new Tyson who is going to be the king of the heavyweights for as long as he wants. Even experienced fight judges wondered whether he could ever be the same again after his three years in prison. It shows that he is a pretty special man when he can climb above that and come back to the ring as good as ever.

I suppose for as long as I live I will think back on the fight and wonder if there was a different way that I could have fought. But the Tyson I met in Las Vegas would, I am sure, have knocked any heavyweight in the world out of his path.

This was the Tyson who knocked Michael Spinks cold in ninety seconds and destroyed Larry Holmes. I thought I was being clever by taking him at the right time. He looked so rusty in his two comeback fights against Peter McNeeley and Buster Mathis that I was confident I could handle him. In my view, he was taking me two or three fights too soon.

But I underestimated the way he has got himself back in shape and into the mood to become the undisputed champion. I cannot see who is going to stop him. Lennox Lewis can make as much noise as he likes, but I do not see him having the ammunition to halt the Tyson march. He can definitely take care of IBF champion Francois Botha, and I would back him to get the better of WBA title-holder Bruce Seldon. Riddick Bowe is one of the best of the other heavyweights around and he just might give Tyson a good fight.

The air was thick with retirement talk when I arrived back in Essex, and one newspaper even went so far as to say that I had decided to quit. That was pure conjecture. I deliberately delayed thinking about my future because I wanted to do it in the peace of my home surrounded by my family. I wanted to talk everything through with Laura and the girls.

I was determined not to make an emotional decision in the heat of the moment like my mate Nigel did. I wanted to chill out at home and arrive at a decision in my own good time. The last thing I wanted was to make the wrong decision, and then start making comebacks like so many other fighters have done in the past, and in particular dear old

Joe Bugner, who was always being linked with me throughout my career.

When it does come my retirement will be final. There will be no comebacks. It will be goodbye boxing, hello the rest of my life.

Sportsmen are a long time retired, and so I am determined to get the timing of my retirement announcement right.

Once I have decided to hang up my gloves you will never find me knocking the fight game. It has opened doors to me that would have always remained closed but for boxing. I have met Queens, Princes, Princesses, Presidents, Prime Ministers and scores of celebrities. The sport has been wonderful to me, and I hope I have managed to put just a little something back. I have always tried to represent my sport and my country with dignity, and I am only sorry that I did not manage to fly the flag the way I wanted to in Las Vegas.

As I sit with my feet up looking out on the green and pleasant English countryside surrounding my home, I look back on the Tyson fight with mixed feelings. I am, and always will be, choked that I did not put up a better show, but I will always be warmed by the memory of the wonderful support I received. As long as I live, I will never forget the reception I got when I climbed into the ring. If it had been Wembley, the noise and the excitement could not have been greater.

It was just unbelievable. Las Vegas has known some pretty wild and wonderful times, but it had never witnessed anything quite like this. From the bottom of my heart I want to thank every single one of those thousands of supporters who dug deep into their pockets to make the trip. I also want to thank the fans who paid to watch it on pay-per-view. They will be able to tell their grandchildren that they saw the first fight shown in Britain on that new system, which I know will have become commonplace and accepted as the norm within a couple of years. It is well established in the United States, and many of the great sporting and show business events take place only because of the support of pay-per-view.

As I reflect on my career, I think warmly of the highlights: taking the European title from the giant Anders Eklund with four successive right uppercuts...knocking Gerrie Coetzee cold with the hardest punch I had ever thrown in a world title eliminator...belting Joe Bugner to defeat after years of having him mock me...and, of course, climbing to the top of the mountain and snatching the world crown from Oliver McCall.

There have been quite a few downers as well, such as my three losing world title challenges, the last-round hammering by Bonecrusher Smith and finally, worst of all, the three round defeat in the return fight with Tyson. But I believe you have to experience the bad to appreciate the good.

Just look around me here to see what I have achieved. Top of the list is my wife and children. They fill me with so much happiness that I could burst. And here in the grounds of my home is something close to paradise. I can come here and chill out without any outside inter-ference, and not having to give interviews here, there and everywhere. Here I am my own man, independent and very very proud.

This is what boxing continues to give me. It is best summed up as p*eace of mind*. I have always had as my main object as a boxer to build a safe and sound future for my family. I think that I have now reached that goal, and I can relax in the knowledge that I have achieved what I set out to do.

I am determined to carry on trying to put something back into life. I have a set number of charities that I am committed to helping in any way that I can, and I will go out of my way to assist wherever possible those less fortunate than me. I am, for instance, very honoured to be an ambassador for the Prince's Trust, and there is much to be done to help and improve the lot of youngsters just starting out on life's demanding road.

I will never forget where I came from. The tough streets in which I grew up prepared me for the life that I have led, and I will always be appreciative of the standards that were set for me by my mother and father. I did not always listen to them when I was a young tearaway, but I now know and understand that all the good advice they kept pouring into my ears was well meant.

Then I was lucky to find myself in a school, as Oak Hall, where there were dedicated teachers who were willing to go beyond the call of duty to help turn wrong 'uns into right 'uns. I was never really going to be the black Ronnie Biggs like I have often joked, but I could have gone down a dodgy old road but for the lessons I learned about respect and discipline at Oak Hall.

Thanks to boxing and those first stumbling interviews with 'Know What I Mean' Harry Carpenter, I got the confidence to appear in front of television cameras and to talk into microphones. I am not pretending that I am the next David Frost or Des Lynam, but I hope and feel that there is some sort of future for me in the media world. Not full-time, but a role that I can fill occasionally and have my little say on things. There has also been talk of a film about my life, nothing concrete but just talk. That would be something I would like to get my teeth into, because, even if I say it myself, I have had a remarkable life and it would give hope to everybody out there who is starting out with nothing.

As I relax in the spring sunshine looking out into the sprouting greenery of deepest Essex, I say a silent prayer of thanks to God for all that I have got and for all that I have achieved. It has not come easily, and I have the bruises to prove it. But Somebody Up There obviously likes me, and I consider myself lucky to have so much go right for me.

So as I take stock of my life and contemplate the future, I start to get the Tyson defeat into context. Now that it is behind me, I can see quite clearly that I was trying for a bridge too far that night in Vegas. It would have been easy for me to have looked for a push-over challenger for my first defence, as so many champions have done in the past. But I was contracted to fight Tyson. I had a deep desire for revenge over the way he had beaten me back in 1989, but it was not to be. Mike Tyson is one of the great heavyweights, and I would suggest that he will add to his growing legend in the months ahead.

I collected a lot of criticism for my performance against Tyson, a lot of it justified. But I want to go on record as saying that in my opinion, based on being on the receiving end of his sledgehammer punches, there is nobody who could have stood up to him that night in Las Vegas.

I failed, and I hold my hands up and admit it. But when the history of this boxing decade is written, it will be noted that I battled with Tyson not once but twice. Believe me, that is something about which I will boast to my grandchildren.

My cut and bruises received in the Tyson fight are now virtually healed, but the pain of defeat will last with me for a long long time. As

I consider my future, there is an ache deep inside me that is telling me that I do not want to end my career on a losing note. Don King has already told me that he could get me a fight for another version of the world championship, and this is a tempting prospect. I want to go out with my head held high when I do eventually decide to retire. There is a lot of thinking to be done, and I do not know of a better place to do it than here in my own personal paradise in a lovely corner of Essex. It's great to be home.

We are now coming to the end of the book on me, Frank Bruno the man, and now you can read about Frank Bruno the fighter with my own personal memories of each contest on the way to the world championship.

It seems a lifetime ago that I started out as a raw novice after just a handful of amateur contests. That was back in the days when I had zero. I just hope I have come out of it all a hero, despite that defeat by Tyson.

PART TWO
The Path to the Title

11 : The Scrapbook

'I could have done without all the hassle before my professional debut. It was hard enough having to concentrate on the fight without worrying about an eye operation and a court case verdict.'

FIGHT No. 1
Opponent: Lupe Guerra (Mexico)
Venue: Royal Albert Hall, London
Date: 17 March 1982
WON by knock out, first round

IT was a starving Frank Bruno who climbed into the ring for his professional debut against Lupe Guerra, a Mexican heavyweight fighting out of Nebraska. He was starving for action. It had been nearly two years since he had last fought when becoming the youngest ever ABA heavyweight champion at the age of eighteen. He had since come through two traumatic experiences that challenged his commitment.

First of all he flew out to Colombia for what was then revolutionary laser treatment to cure short-sightedness in his right eye after the British Boxing Board of Control had turned down his application for a licence. Then he became embroiled in a legal tug of war as to exactly who managed him. It was Terry Lawless who paid for him to go to Colombia for the operation, but Essex businessman Burt McCarthy had talked him into signing a letter of intent that he lodged with the Board as evidence that he was his manager. McCarthy applied for an injunction to try to stop Bruno fighting under Lawless.

Just two days before his debut the High Court judge threw out the injunction, ruling that Lawless held the only valid contract with Bruno, who was described in court as 'a hot property'. But there was a sting in the tail. The judge ruled when coming down on the side of Lawless that McCarthy could eventually be entitled to substantial damages, which was to prove expensively true at a later date.

All Bruno wanted to do was concentrate on his new career as a professional fighter...

I could have done without all the hassle before my debut. It was nerve racking enough without having to worry about an eye operation and a court case. I wanted to be focused on my boxing without any distractions, and was happy to start my career with Terry. I was just a naive youngster when McCarthy, who drove me around in a flash yellow Rolls Royce, talked me into signing the piece of paper that caused all the trouble. He turned my head and I became confused. Who wouldn't have been in similar circumstances?

My knees were wobbling before I made my debut against Guerra. I had been given a big build-up in the press and there was a lot of pressure on me. I wasn't worried so much about the fight but about not letting people down. I knew a lot was expected of me and it made me nervous. Now I look back, I'm sure that Guerra had been carefully picked but that is surely sensible matchmaking. It has been claimed that Rocky Marciano's manager went to the extreme of putting him in with relatives in his early contests! In boxing terms I was still a novice. I had boxed only twenty-one times as an amateur, and I'd managed to reverse my one defeat by an Irish charmer called Joe Christle.

I first met Guerra at the weigh-in. He had a worn face that looked as if it had been on the end of a lot of punches. He was shorter than me by about three inches and when he caught sight of me walking stripped to the scales I could see a sudden flicker of doubt in his eyes. I had already got myself into good physical shape that made opponents realise I had not been training for a game of marbles. Boxing's a serious business, and from day one I was always determined to be properly prepared, both physically and mentally.

I shook Guerra's hand just before going onto the scales, and he gave me a half smile that changed into a snarl as he seemed to remember that I was the man he would be fighting a few hours later. I already knew the importance of appearing confident and self-assured at weigh-ins. It is a vital part of the psychological warfare. I try not to be cocky and flash but make sure that I ooze confidence. My boyhood hero Muhammad Ali used to turn a weigh-in into a sideshow. It was part ticket-selling hype, but his act was also designed to make his opponent feel inferior as if he was there just for a walk-on part.

I weighed in at just half a pound under fifteen-and-a-half stone and had a twenty-one pound weight advantage over Lupe, who had won seventeen of his twenty-three professional fights. On paper it looked as if he could give me a good test. 'Nice and cool, Frank,' Terry Lawless said as I waited for the first bell of my professional career. 'Open him up with your jab and just take your time. Be lucky.' As the timekeeper shouted 'seconds out' all my nerves disappeared and I felt in complete control of myself. This was the moment I had been dreaming about for years. Frank Bruno, professional boxer. Suddenly I was out into the centre of the ring, jabbing with my left in the way that I had practised thousands of times in the gymnasium. Now this was for real.

Guerra came at me aggressively and got through my defence with a couple of quick left leads of his own before coming in close and holding my right arm in a vice-like grip. Referee Paddy Sower pushed us apart, and I was surprised to find that Guerra had switched from an orthodox stance to southpaw. Barely a minute of the fight had gone and already he was trying old pro tricks that were new to me. I managed to connect with my first full-power combination, a left-right to the head, and I felt him wobble. He grabbed my gloves and I had to wrestle him off me. His legs were shaky and he stumbled to the canvas. I went to a neutral corner and watched Guerra scrambling on his hands and knees as the referee counted over him. I looked to my own corner where Terry was miming a left lead.

Guerra got up at eight and came towards me with his head down. I shaped to throw a left jab but changed it to an uppercut and he immediately dropped back to the canvas. After another eight count, Guerra showed he was still a danger as he attempted to throw a desperate haymaker as I walked in behind a long left jab. I let rip with the sort of four-punch combination to the head that I had been learning in the gym. They all landed on target. Good solid shots. Guerra fell backwards in a heap to the canvas, and I knew from the look on his face that this time there was no chance of him beating the count. It was all over with just under half a minute of the round to go.

I looked down at the BBC ringside commentator who was giving me the thumbs-up sign. It was Desmond Lynam, know what I mean! Harry Carpenter had another appointment that night. It was one of the few fights of mine that he missed.

FIGHT No. 2
Opponent: Harvey Steichen (USA)
Venue: Wembley Arena, London
Date: 30 March 1982
WON by stoppage, second round

FOR his second professional fight, Frank returned to Wembley Arena almost two years to the day since he had won the ABA heavyweight title in the same ring in 1980. Waiting for him in the opposite corner was Harvey Steichen, a stocky, barrel-chested American from Carson City who looked to be carrying a tyre around his waist. He had an excess of weight and also of confidence. 'You're gonna be in big trouble tonight, Bruno,' he said at the weigh-in. 'I'm gonna bust your ass.'

I knew just by looking at Steichen that he was hardly a fitness fanatic. He tipped the scales at a couple of pounds over sixteen stone, and I was going to have to give away nearly a stone. But I felt the extra weight was going to handicap him, because he did not look to me as if he would be very mobile. My fight plan to was keep the opening exchanges at long range, and I kept my left jabs queuing on the end of Steichen's broad nose in the first round. He was an unconventional fighter who threw swinging punches from odd angles. I just kept stepping inside them and banging my left in as straight and as hard as I could. By the end of the first round I noticed that Steichen was beginning to breathe heavily and his face had gone a dull shade of red from where my left fist was landing. He seemed to have aged several years as he returned to his corner, and I had not yet let go any of my heavy ammunition. Steichen swung an out-of-range left early in the second round and I saw the chance to cross with my right. It landed with a downward chopping effect on the side of his head, and as he staggered sideways I followed up with a left hook that dropped him onto his knees in my own corner. He got up at five and came swinging at me wildly. I threw four successive rights, none of which connected with full force but the power was enough to send him falling face first to the canvas. Referee Harry Gibbs counted to nine, and as Steichen got up he cuddled both arms around him and led him to his corner.

FIGHT No. 3
Opponent: Tom Stevenson (USA)
Venue: Royal Albert Hall, London
Date: 20 April 1982
WON by knockout, first round

O N paper, Frank's third opponent looked as if he could give him a tough test. But in the ring, Tom Stevenson did not live up to his pre-fight billing or to his boasting. The man from Indianapolis had won seven of his twelve professional contests and had a reputation for being a dangerous one-hit knockout puncher. But as it turned out he proved no match for Bruno, and he surrendered so tamely that for the first time in his career Frank heard boos from a dissatisfied crowd.

I really got myself keyed up for the fight because I thought I was in for a hard night's work. At fourteen stone eight pounds Stevenson was giving me ten pounds. At the weigh-in he looked to have a good build on him and appeared to have all the confidence in the world. 'I have not come all this way to lose,' he told newspaper reporters. 'I've never heard of this guy Bruno but he's sure going to know all about me.' All I found out about him was that he seemed not to want to fight. He hid behind a high guard and hardly threw a punch as I stalked him, wondering what tactical plan he was trying. He stabbed out a couple of lefts that fell well short, and when I rammed three stiff jabs to the head his eyes opened wide as if to say: 'Hell, if this is his left jab what's his right like?'

Stevenson soon found out. I threw a long right hook that landed high up on his temple. He retreated back to the ropes as I followed up with a full-blooded left-right combination that landed on his gloves which he had cupped to his face. The force of my punches lifted him backwards and through the middle rope onto the ring apron. There were jeers and boos from the crowd as Stevenson sat on the ring apron, making little effort to get back through the ropes as referee Larry O'Connell counted him out. I was as frustrated as the fans. It was not my fault that he had no heart for the fight, but the booing was a warning sign that the public would not stand for me being fed soft touches.

FIGHT No. 4
Opponent: Ron Gibbs (USA)
Venue: Wembley Arena, London
Date: 4 May 1982
WON by stoppage, fourth round

THERE was now pressure on manager Terry Lawless to agree to a step up in the standard of Frank's opponents following the abysmal surrender of Tom Stevenson. His argument that Frank was still at the 'L-plates' stage of his career after just four rounds of professional boxing following a relatively short amateur career found little support among Fleet Street's ringside experts. Ron Gibbs, with a reasonable record of durability, was called in from Nevada as test number four.

For three rounds I struggled to get into my rhythm against Gibbs, a slippery customer with good balance. He was the classiest fighter I had met to date and he frustrated me by clever use of the ring. My left jab wasn't landing with its usual power and accuracy. He was a master at parrying my lead, and then shooting over fast right counters that really tested my defence. If you're wondering how I've got such good recall of the action from each of my fights it's because I have a video collection of all my professional contests, and I used to watch them for hours on end to analyse myself and figure out where I could improve and sharpen my punch combinations and my all-round ring strategy.

I look back now at those first three rounds against Gibbs and I'm almost embarrassed. I can't believe that I used to be so stiff and tense. I got careless early in the fourth round, and he startled me with an uppercut that clipped me on the chin. He then dropped his right ready for another crack and I let a left hook go with a full pivot of my shoulder and hips, turning my wrist to get a corkscrew effect at the moment of impact. It was as good a punch as I had thrown and Gibbs fell sideways into the ropes. Gibbs amazed me by just managing to beat the count, and I was relieved when referee Roland Dakin moved in to save him before I could unload any more really damaging punches. I was happy with that final punch, but the first three rounds were unsatisfactory. There was still, I knew, a lot for me to learn about the professional game.

114

FIGHT No. 5
Opponent: Tony Moore (GB)
Venue: Royal Albert Hall, London
Date: 1 June 1982
WON by stoppage, second round

TONY Moore was a vastly experienced, have-gloves-will-travel professional who had journeyed all over the world from his Hendon, Middlesex, base. He had shared the ring with some of the finest heavyweights around, rarely beating the top-line fighters, but always giving a good account of himself in what were usually distance fights. Moore was noted for having a strong chin, and many thought that with the right backing he could have become a power on the world stage. He was coming up for his fifty-fourth fight, compared to the five for Frank. Most good judges predicted that Moore would give Frank a thorough examination.

Moore, who I knew and liked, was convinced that I was making a mistake taking him on. He couldn't forget that I had sparred with him during my amateur days, and still thought of me as that baby he used to mess around with in the gym. But the baby had grown up! I had always found Tony a nice, approachable man, but he made it clear that there was no room for friendship leading up to our fight. He gave me quite a bit of verbal punishment, and said that he did not think I deserved the publicity build-up that I was getting and made no secret of the fact that he was going to put me in my place. In his view, he should have had the sort of headlines that were coming my way. He insisted that he was a class above me, and said that 'the Bruno bubble is about to burst'.

Moore was a wise old pro and I realised that the things he was saying were meant to make me jittery, but I just turned a deaf ear to them and worked extra hard in training. He was my first domestic opponent and I knew the media would watch the fight closely because they were going to be able to measure me against a fighter whose form and record they knew. I could not believe the amount of publicity I was getting after just a handful of fights, and everybody seemed to want to have a say as to what sort of opponents I should be facing. To read some of the criticism, you would have thought I was a veteran of fifty fights rather than a virtual novice with just four fights behind me. Moore was convinced that he was going to show me that I still had a lot to learn.

Although having lost twenty-four of his contests, he was noted for being an iron man of the ring who usually managed to go the full distance. But he seemed to lose his heart for the fight within the first minute, after I had softened him up with a few full-power left jabs which I threw with all my shoulder weight behind them. He became very apprehensive and tried to smother and hold rather than let his own punches go.

I was surprised that a man of Tony's vast experience should keep going back on to the ropes Muhammad Ali-style, making himself an easy target for my punches. Maybe he was trying to lure me on to one of his favourite left hooks, but I was not going to fall for that. When the bell ended the first round I had already given him a good tanking by trapping him on the ropes. As I walked back to my corner I knew, without being flash, that he was not going to give me the distance experience that I needed.

At fifteen stone five pounds I had a weight advantage of just over a stone, and I made full use of it in the second round. I forced him back and unleashed a long left-right-left combination that I had been practising in the gym. It was a left jab, right cross and left hook - all thrown with maximum power and each punch landing to the head.

Poor old Tony went down like a sack of potatoes, not knowing whether it was Christmas or Easter. He bravely dragged himself up at nine but fell back against the ropes, and as I moved forward to complete my night's work referee Sid Nathan jumped in between us to save Moore from a bigger hiding.

Back in the calm and safety of the dressing-room Tony, disappointed that he had not been allowed to give a better showing against me, announced that he was hanging up his gloves. He'd had a long, twelve-year career and with better guidance might have gone right to the top. I wished him a long and happy retirement. He deserved it. This was easily the most satisfying win of my career to date. The victory gave me a confidence boost, and I was now anxious for a step up in class. But my manager Terry Lawless – as throughout most of my time under his guidance – preached patience.

FIGHT No. 6
Opponent: George Scott (GB)
Venue: Wembley Arena, London
Date: 14 September 1982
WON by stoppage, first round

D URING the summer of 1982 Frank was taken on his first learning trip to the United States. He trained and sparred in gymnasiums in New York, Los Angeles and Las Vegas and really got the flavour of the big fight game in America. Most memorable for him was working out in California with Mike Weaver, who was then the reigning WBA champion. On his return home Frank planned to put into practise what he had learned against Geordie George Scott, a former Northern Area heavyweight champion from Newcastle.

According to his record, Scott was strong and durable. He certainly talked a good fight, and promised to end my unbeaten run. At the weigh-in I scaled my heaviest-ever fifteen stone eight pounds, but I was still having to give a couple of pounds to Scott who also had a slight height and reach advantage. He was known as the 'King of Geordieland', and he reckoned that I would have to bow the knee to him. But he just froze the moment the first bell went, and he must know in his heart that he let himself down against me.

It was all over in the first round and I can't recollect him hitting me with a single punch. He seemed to lose interest from the moment I threw an uppercut through the middle of his defence and jolted his head back. The punch landed as I drove him towards my own corner, and he sank to the canvas and took an eight count. I could sense that he was already a beaten man. He had a hunted look in his eyes but in the ring there's no place to hide. Scott retreated to the ropes and I practised my combinations. A solid, straight left, then a follow-through right, a left uppercut, right cross and finally a big left hook that sent him back to the canvas. He made it obvious that he had taken enough when he got up at eight. As I moved forward he ducked his head behind his gloves, leaving referee Sid Nathan with no alternative but to stop it. Scott suddenly wanted to be a million miles away.

FIGHT No. 7
Opponent: Ali Lukusa (Zaire)
Venue: West Berlin Sportshalle, Germany
Date: 23 October 1982
WON by knock out, second round

FRANK went to Berlin for his seventh fight as manager Terry Lawless tried to ease the weight of expectancy that was like a sack of coal on Bruno's back every time he climbed into the ring. People were expecting mature performances from him even though his entire professional career to date had lasted less than twelve rounds. The German promoters came up with what promised to be a searching test from the strong and experienced Ali Lukusa, who was born in Zaire and boxed out of Spain where he was highly regarded both for his skill and power.

My fight plan was to make a cautious start, working behind my left jab while I sussed out what Lukusa was made of. He was taller and heavier than me and tried to dance out of range in a sort of Muhammad Ali style. The idea of trying to get some rounds under my belt quickly went out of the window when I made Lukusa wobble with the first serious punch that I threw. I then decided to go for a quick finish. I cut off his escape route as he danced backwards around the ring by trapping him in a corner. Two left hooks to the body and a right to the head dropped him for a nine count. He launched a two-fisted attack as soon as he got up, but I stepped inside his long reach and toppled him again with an overarm right to the side of the head. As he again rose at nine the bell rang. Lukusa came out for the second round with his hands held high, and he tried to stop me setting myself for an attack by crowding me. I let him come to me and then buried a left hook just above the waistband on his shorts. As he bent double I brought an uppercut sweeping from hip level. It got him right on the point of the jaw and he fell at my feet as if he had been shot. The ten-second count was a formality. My first experience of fighting overseas could not have gone better. It was just not Lukusa's night. He was mugged on the way back to his hotel.

FIGHT No. 8
Opponent: Rudi Gauwe (Belgium)
Venue: Royal Albert Hall, London
Date: 9 November 1982
WON by stoppage, second round

B ELGIAN Rudi Gauwe came in as a late substitute for Austrian Helmut Owessle, which signalled a sudden step up in the quality of opposition for Frank. Gauwe was no stranger to the Royal Albert Hall. He had fought there in 1980 when John L Gardner, then a member of the Terry Lawless stable, forced him to retire after nine rounds of a fight for the vacant European championship.

Gauwe was the most experienced of all my opponents to date. Everybody seemed convinced that he would give me a much-needed taste of going several rounds. At fifteen stone six pounds I had a four pound weight advantage, and I noticed at the weigh-in that Gauwe looked a bit thick around the waist. I made up my mind that I would go for his body, and I quickly discovered that this was the way to unsettle him. Each time I landed in the first round with two-fisted attacks to the ribs he grunted like a winded pig and he was puffing and panting as he returned to his corner at the bell.

My self-confidence was growing all the time. Looking back at the video of the fight it's interesting to see that I was much more relaxed and loose-limbed than in my early contests when I was too stiff and upright. I was at last producing my gymnasium form in the ring.

The first punch of the second round, a stiff left jab, split the bridge of Gauwe's nose. I then followed on with an overarm right to the side of the jaw and he fell backwards with his right leg twisting under him. He was almost crying with pain as referee Sid Nathan counted him out, and when he finally got up he limped heavily back to his corner. The crowd booed him, but I think they would have been more sympathetic had they realised he had broken an ankle when he went down. Joe Bugner, who had just started a comeback campaign, was sitting at the ringside with promoter Frank Warren ready with a challenge. But boxing politics would keep us apart for another five years.

FIGHT No. 9
Opponent: Georg Butzbach (Germany)
Venue: Wembley Arena, London
Date: 23 November 1982
WON, retired first round

R AY Clarke, British Boxing Board of Control secretary, lit the fuse to a Frank Bruno controversy after he had scored his ninth successive inside-the-distance victory. Clarke announced: 'Now the honeymoon is over. Bruno must in future meet men with more experience and of more substance.' Manager Terry Lawless told the Press: 'All of Frank's opponents have been thoroughly vetted by the Board. It is not our fault that they become so intimidated by Bruno that they refuse to fight on the night. If the Board try to make me put him in with men that I consider are over his head, we will pack our bags and go to the States. There he can get the experience he needs without the inquests. This country has been crying out for a world heavyweight champion since the beginning of the century. Now we have suddenly found a boy who might make it one day we should be bending over backwards to protect him as much possible.' This angry exchange was triggered by Frank's hasty first round victory over German heavyweight Georg Butzbach.

Butzbach, who weighed five-and-a-half pounds less than me at fifteen stone, looked to have an inviting stomach and I decided as early as at the weigh-in to make it my target. He rushed out obviously looking for a quick finish. I made sure he got it! Butzbach came charging forward with his elbows out. I arched to my left and sent a left corkscrewing into the pit of his stomach. The German yelled out with pain and sank to the canvas. He took a count of seven on one knee and was obviously struggling to catch his breath. The punch had knocked all of the wind out of him and when he got up he turned his back on me and raised an arm in surrender. It went down into the record books as a first-round retirement. This was the best body punch I had ever thrown, but there were boos from back-of-the-hall fans who did not realise just how much it had hurt Butzbach.

FIGHT No. 10
Opponent: Gilberto Acuna (Puerto Rico)
Venue: Royal Albert Hall, London
Date: 7 December, 1982
WON by stoppage, first round

IT was a British Boxing Board of Control official who recommended Gilberto Acuna as a suitable opponent for Frank's tenth fight. He had won twelve of his twenty professional contests and had lasted six rounds against Joe Bugner in Los Angeles in 1980. Against Frank, he lasted just forty seconds. It was the final fight of his 1982 programme. Ten fights, ten wins, all inside the distance and they had lasted less than seventeen rounds in total.

I do not feel I was given the credit I deserved for my instant victory over Acuna. I have watched the video recording of the fight time and again, and I know that the punch that finished the fight would have troubled any heavyweight in the world. The fact that it was the only serious punch of the fight meant the fans did not feel they had got value for their money, but I was delighted to get it over and done with in such style. I threw a light left lead and then a measured right cross to the side of the head and Acuna crashed backwards to the canvas. He was up at six, but his legs were wobbling and referee Harry Gibbs signalled that he had seen enough.

Board of Control secretary Ray Clarke said after the quickest win of my career that he was 'not altogether happy' about the match, yet the Board had given the contest their blessing after one of their stewards had seen Acuna knock out Eddie Cooper at Walthamstow. There was a lot of booing from the fans, who obviously felt that Acuna could have carried on. But, believe me, he was in no fit state to defend himself. I have had the power of my right-hand punch tested by scientists who reported that when I'm letting it go at full power it travels at more than twenty miles an hour and lands with a force of half a ton. It was travelling at top speed when I connected with Acuna's face. The punch scattered his senses and when he got up his legs betrayed him with a sort of delayed impact effect. Harry Gibbs was right to step in.

FIGHT No. 11
Opponent: Stewart Lithgo (GB)
Venue: Royal Albert Hall, London
Date: 18 January 1983
WON, retired fourth round

STEWART Lithgo stirred an ingredient of spice into the build-up for Frank's first fight of 1983. He was convinced he had been fed a diet of pushovers and made no secret of the fact that he was going to give him a good hiding. Lithgo, an ex-jump jockey who had outgrown his sport, was the 25-year-old Northern Area champion from Hartlepool. Since turning professional in 1979 he had won fourteen fights, drawn one and lost three. He was unbeaten in his first thirteen fights and earned himself a place in a British title eliminator against Gordon Ferris who hammered him to defeat in two rounds. He now saw the chance of re-establishing himself as a title contender by knocking Frank out of his path. Lithgo wasn't exactly short of confidence. He told the trade paper *Boxing News*: 'I don't think Bruno is anything special at all. He hasn't fought anybody yet. In fact he hasn't even been hit. He's been knocking over selling platers. The wife could have knocked out the last two mugs he met. Bruno may have been billed as the great British hope but I intend to knock him down to size.'

Lithgo missed the weigh-in because his train from Hartlepool was delayed, and so I didn't see him until we climbed into the Albert Hall ring. When he took off his dressing-gown I couldn't believe what a beanpole build he had. He was as tall as me but scaled only thirteen stone ten pounds and was the lightest of all my opponents. There was no love lost between us after all the nasty things that he had said, and I went out with the intention of beating him in style. But I found him a really awkward cuss to fight and I gave what I reckon was the least impressive performance of my career.

I've got to give Lithgo full credit. He fought as if his life depended on it, and there were times when he put me under a lot of pressure with long, swinging punches that didn't hurt me but made me cover up and protect myself behind a high guard. I found the range with my left jab after a quiet opening round and made his nose bleed with four good stiff jabs. This would have knocked the heart out of many fighters, but Lithgo gritted his teeth and launched a two-fisted attack that had me defending myself for the longest spell since I had turned professional. I thought I had put his lights out early in the third round when I caught him with a nicely timed right cross. His lanky frame shook as if he was suddenly standing on moving ground, but instead of falling over he came swarming all over me with his arms going like windmill sails.

About halfway through the round I threw a right hook that opened a nasty gash on Lithgo's cheekbone, just below the left eye. Then I made him grunt with a left hook to the body and a right uppercut to the chin. He took a backward step and came back fighting, and we were standing toe to toe swapping punches when the bell rang to end the round. I boxed more coolly in the fourth round and kept Lithgo on the end of my jab. Several of my right hooks thudded against the cut on his cheekbone and I could see that it was now spreading up and around his left eye. A lot of the power had drained from his punches but he was still dangerous and keen to have a go. As the bell ended the fourth round I sensed that I was not far away from victory. But it came quicker than I expected because his corner retired him after referee Sid Nathan had been called over to inspect the deep cut by his eye.

It was a wise decision although Lithgo didn't think so. He was furious when his manager Dennie Mancini retired him, and I thought that for a moment he was going to start another fight in his own corner. Speaking selfishly I would have liked to have had one more round because I am convinced I could have knocked him down. He was the first opponent never to have taken a count against me and so I suppose that was a victory of some sort for him. I normally exchange some friendly words with my opponents at the end of a fight but Lithgo didn't want to know. 'You're still nothing,' he snarled before leaving the ring for stitching treatment to his cut. I shrugged and returned to the dressing-room where I told the newspaper reporters that while Lithgo was one of the gamest fighters I had ever met he had not managed to hurt me once. I could have told them about how a bad cold had held up my training programme and almost led to a postponement, but I didn't want anybody to think I was making excuses. All in all, a fight to forget.

FIGHT No. 12
Opponent: Peter Mulendwa (Uganda)
Venue: Royal Albert Hall, London
Date: 8 February 1983
WON by knock out, round three

FRANK was as excited as a little kid on his birthday when told the name of the opponent for his first top-of-the-bill contest: Alfredo Evangelista. The former European champion would give him a real step-up in class. This Uruguayan-born, Spanish-based boxer had made two challenges for the world heavyweight championship, going the distance with a past-his-peak Muhammad Ali and getting knocked out in seven rounds by Larry Holmes. Frank collected every single fight video of Evangelista in action that he could lay his hands on and studied him for hours until he felt he knew his style almost as well as he knew his own.

You can imagine how deflated I felt when seventy-two hours before the fight Evangelista pulled out with a wrist injury. Peter Mulendwa, a Ugandan based in Italy, was called in as substitute, and along with many people I said, 'Who?' When we came face to face at the weigh-in I just couldn't believe how small he looked. Mulendwa weighed the same as Stewart Lithgo but was nowhere near as tall. I was on a real hiding to nothing. If I beat him, the press were going to say 'so what?'. If I lost it would be a disaster. After two rounds softening him up with jabs I increased the pace and the power of my punches, and I could sense him running out of steam. Suddenly, midway through the third, I unleashed one of the body punches I had been saving for Evangelista. It was a right hook and Mulendwa gasped as I sunk it deep beneath his ribs. He tried to fall forward into a clinch but I backed away ready to toss in some head punches. He couldn't hide the effect of the body shot, and he suddenly reeled away from me and sprawled in his own corner clutching his gloves to his stomach. Referee Harry Gibbs counted the sorry-looking Mulendwa out. To be honest, he just did not belong in the same ring as me. I hope that doesn't sound flash. It's just fact. I felt really frustrated by it all.

FIGHT No. 13
Opponent: Winston Allen (GB)
Venue: Royal Albert Hall, London
Date: 1 March 1983
WON by stoppage, second round

JOE Bugner's comeback had pumped new interest into the heavyweight division and the air was thick with talk of a showdown with Bruno. Much of the talk was being done by Joe's outspoken Australian wife, Marlene. There was a view that Joe might have become world champion if he could have fought half as aggressively as she talked. Frank was ready to fight Joe. Any time, any place. But Terry Lawless was still preaching the virtue of patience. There was also a political wall between the two boxers. Bugner was in the camp of Frank Warren, who had arrived on the scene as a rival to the long-established Mickey Duff-Jarvis Astaire-Mike Barrett team. Bugner kept stirring the pot by making cracks about the way Frank was being groomed. 'He is being fed fighters I wouldn't hire as sparring partners,' he said. 'The only reason he won't agree to fight me is that he knows that he will be stepping out of his class. What is he going to learn by fighting opponents who can't lay a glove on him?' Winston Allen, a black Welshman from Swansea, was booked as Frank's thirteenth opponent.

I have to admit that Joe Bugner was bugging me. He was one of the best defensive boxers in the world, no question of that. He had twice gone the distance with Ali, had outpointed Henry Cooper, had given Joe Frazier a hard time in a distance fight and was noted for the toughness of his chin. But he was also one of the most boring of all heavyweights to watch because his style was so negative. I would have jumped at the chance to test Joe's chin with my right hand, but I had to make do with trying to show that anything he could do I could do better. It took him six rounds to beat Gilberto Acuna. I managed it in forty seconds. In his comeback campaign he had stopped Winston Allen in three rounds after looking in a bit of bother, and he stopped Eddie Neilson on cuts in five rounds. Now it was my turn to take on Allen, and if I could beat him then southpaw Neilson was next in line.

Allen was reckoned to be one of the hardest hitting heavyweights around. He had used his flashing right fist to score one-round knockout victories over Stan McDermott and former European champion Jean-Pierre Coopmans, and he had shown durability in going the distance with powerful punchers David Pearce and Alfredo Evangelista. I made a careful video study of Allen and was concerned at the dangerous way he used his head. He often butted like a billy goat, and Joe Bugner complained about his tactics during their fight and also claimed that Allen had at one stage bitten him. I've heard of hungry fighters but that's ridiculous!

Before the fight, staged on St David's Day, there had been a lot of discussion in the media as to whether or not I could take a punch to the chin. Allen, they said, had the punching power to test me. What would happen if he bounced his big right hand against my chin? The answer came within less than a minute of the opening round. Allen threw a looping right that landed flush on my jaw. It felt as if I'd had an electric shock and I took a step backwards. From then on I was on red alert, and I kept Allen under pressure from a bombardment of left jabs that had him running round the ring in a bid to escape. Jab, jab, jab into his face and then thumping rights into his ribs as he tried holding me to stop the leather pouring into his face. I was more tense than I like to be, but Allen was made for my straight left and he was almost eating it. He hung on at every opportunity, and referee James Brimmell briefly stopped the action while he warned Allen to stop holding. By the bell at the end of the first round I knew that I had his measure.

Predictably, Allen threw that right of his as he came out at the start of the second. He might just as well have sent me a postcard to say it was coming. I stepped inside it and powered two stiff left jabs in and then two clubbing rights to the side of his head. Then I tried a short right hook that hit him high on the temple and he stumbled sideways. A left cross pulled him upright in his tracks and then I followed on with a heavy right that shook him from head to toe. I was getting ready to unload my biggest bombs when he suddenly turned his back on me. It was a total surrender and referee James Brimmell wrestled me away and raised my hand before I could let any more punches go. I had the satisfaction of beating Allen in quicker time and more impressively than Joe Bugner, and I had proved I could take a punch.

FIGHT No 14
Opponent: Eddie Neilson (GB)
Venue: Royal Albert Hall, London
Date: 5 April 1983
WON by stoppage, third round

LIKE Joe Bugner, Eddie Neilson had a wife who could talk a good fight. She gave Frank a lot of verbal hammer before he and her husband finally settled their differences in the ring. An interesting fight would have been Mrs Bugner versus Mrs Neilson! A West Country fighter from Swindon, Neilson was Frank's first southpaw opponent. He was a dangerous puncher who had been more than holding his own against Joe Bugner until stopped with cuts in five rounds.

I'll say this for Eddie, he was as brave as a lion. Anybody with less courage would not have come out for the second round after I had given him a terrible hammering in the first three minutes. In the opening seconds I landed with a left-right combination to the head. They were not full-blast punches, but there was enough power behind them to topple Eddie to the canvas. He got up too quickly and tried to come in close as I rocked him with punches from long range. I met him with short hooks and uppercuts and he was back on the canvas, this time for a count of eight. Eddie ducked low and came charging at me with a brave counter-attack, but a right cross had him touching down on one knee for a count of two. As he went back to his corner at the end of the round he had a slight trickle of blood coming from around his right eye.

I deliberately slowed down the pace in the second round, continually stopping Neilson in his tracks with solid lefts jabs. He came bulldozing at me in the third round in his brave but reckless style, and as I moved back towards the ropes I fired a looping right hook that travelled in a wide arc before landing just above his right eye. He went down on his knees, screwing up his face with pain. Blood started to spurt from above his right eye and referee Sid Nathan immediately waved the fight over. Once again I had the satisfaction of winning in quicker time and much more convincingly than Bugner.

FIGHT No. 15
Opponent: Scott LeDoux (USA)
Venue: Wembley Arena, London
Date: 3 May 1983
WON on a stoppage, round three

SCOTT LeDoux, a brawler from Minnesota, had been in with the very best heavyweights around. He held both Ken Norton and Leon Spinks to draws, was narrowly outpointed over twelve rounds by Mike Weaver and went seven rounds with Larry Holmes in a 1980 challenge for the WBC crown. He promised to provide Frank with a tough test.

During the build-up to the fight, former world heavyweight champion Floyd Patterson had spent some time in the Royal Oak gymnasium showing the value of getting my shoulder behind the jab. I got the feeling that Floyd was not all that impressed when he watched me sparring, but he had become a 'Bruno believer' by the time he had witnessed my fight with LeDoux from a ringside seat at Wembley.

LeDoux weighed in at sixteen stone two pounds and had a six-and-a-half pound weight advantage. He didn't look built for speed, and so I went out with the intention of setting a fast pace. I found it easy to pick him off with the jab as he retreated with a crab-like style, suddenly launching counter attacks that were, to be honest, surprisingly crude for a fighter of his vast experience. I dropped him for a count of five in the first round, and I could see the confidence almost visibly draining out of him.

He tried to rough me up at close quarters in the second, using his head as a third glove. Referee Larry O'Connell was quick to spot him trying to butt me and warned him. I found a better way to warn him. I whacked him with a right hook that landed just above his left eye and split the eyebrow. LeDoux started the third round with a desperate two-fisted attack, and he managed to get through my defence with a left hook that acted as a warning to me not to get careless. I went back to my first-round policy of throwing plenty of heavy left jabs and blood started to pour from the injured eye as LeDoux's head was continually jolted back. It was such a bad cut that the referee had no option but to stop the fight.

FIGHT No. 16
Opponent: Barry Funches (USA)
Venue: Royal Albert Hall, London
Date: 31 May 1983
WON on a stoppage, round five

F RANK had been mentally preparing himself for a showdown with Joe Bugner, but boxing politics had for the time being killed off any chance of them getting together in the same ring. Waiting for him in the opposite corner instead was Barry Funches, a punching postman from New York who had featured on the Wembley Arena bill against former British champion Gordon Ferris when Frank made his second appearance as a professional. Ferris beat Funches on points over eight rounds.

I followed strict orders not to go for a quick finish because it was felt that I needed some experience of going several rounds. Some of the critics had been dismissing Barry Funches as 'strictly an opponent', whose professional record was dotted with defeats. But they were not having to climb into the ring with him, and I approached the fight with my usual single-mindedness and concentration.

At fifteen stone seven pounds I had a stone weight advantage, and right from the first bell I was fully in command. For four rounds I hardly had my left jab out of his face. I was concentrating on pacing myself, and deliberately held back with my big bombs.

Everything went to plan, and I was let off the leash as we approached the halfway stage of the fight. It was unknown territory for me when I went out at the start of the fifth because it was the first time that I had gone past the fourth round. I opened with another procession of left jabs just to make Funches think that it was going to be the same pattern as before. Then I stepped in sharply and threw a right uppercut that jolted his head back. His legs splayed and as he started falling to the canvas I followed on with a right hook. Funches just beat the count, but was stumbling like a man on rubber legs. I landed two more rights that sent him reeling sideways before referee Harry Gibbs stepped in and led Funches back to his corner.

FIGHT No. 17
Opponent: Mike Jameson (USA)
Venue: De Vinci Manor, Chicago
Date: 15 July 1983
WON by knock out, second round

AS part of Frank's educational trip to the United States in the summer of 1983 he was matched with Mike Jameson, a former nightclub bouncer from California. His American debut took place in the unusual setting of the Chicago De Vinci Manor, a plush dance hall that was decorated with chandeliers and marble statues. The fight was staged in the afternoon so that it could be screened 'live' in Britain by BBCTV. Chicago is known as the Windy City, but the fight went on in the middle of a heatwave. It was like a furnace in the ring under the scorching combination of the television and ring lights. Jameson had been a late starter as a professional boxer, switching from American football at the age of twenty-five. He had got his career off to an impressive start with a string of victories and his first-round win against Ron Gibbs, one of Frank's former opponents, was evidence that he could bang a bit. Jameson then hit a losing run, and he made no secret of the fact that he saw a victory over Bruno as a quick way of getting himself back into the reckoning as a potential contender.

Like a lot of United States heavyweights Jameson was curious to know more about me after I had been named 'Prospect of the Year' by *Ring* magazine, which is the 'bible' of American boxing. I was in terrific shape for the contest after working out for ten days at the Grossinger's Camp in New York State where I had sparred with highly rated heavyweights James 'Quick' Tillis, Jeff Sims and an unknown youngster called Mike Tyson. We were showing off the 'Best of British' to the Americans. British champions Barry McGuigan and my stablemate at the time, Lloyd Honeyghan, were also on the bill. Barry impressed everybody with his power and finesse when he knocked out his first American opponent, Lavon McGowan, in the first round. Honeyghan survived a first-round knock down to fight back and stop Kevin Austin in the tenth and final round of a really hectic welterweight scrap. It's worth noting here that Barry, Lloyd and, finally, myself, went on to win world titles, so the Americans really were seeing some extra special prospects. After Barry and Lloyd had done their bit, I was determined not to let the British side down.

Jameson came into the ring for our fight with a thick growth of beard, which used to be illegal, and he looked as if he had stepped out of a Hammer Horror film. But all the horrors were to be his. I started cautiously behind a straight left and Jameson retreated, hiding his face behind a high guard. The Californian kept peeping at me between his gloves looking for an opening to launch a counter-attack. Every time he shaped to throw a punch I just filled his face with my left glove, drilling in solid jabs and hooks. Jameson had a complete change of tactics in the second round, charging at me with both fists swinging. Very deliberately, I threw what was my best combination of punches to date. I saw him lower his right and I unleashed a left hook to the point of his jaw, delivering it with a full turn of my hips. The effect on Jameson was startling. His right leg came up off the canvas as if he had trodden on broken glass. He was falling sideways towards the canvas when I almost straightened him up with a right uppercut that was stage two of my combination. The punch came up from round about my knees, and as it landed under his chin he crashed backwards, out to the world.

Angelo Dundee, the ace trainer who had been chief cornerman for Muhammad Ali and Sugar Ray Leonard among many other kings of the ring, told reporters: 'This is the best heavyweight prospect from Britain in a long, long time. He's got the sort of natural punching power that will cause problems for any heavyweight in the world. But having said that, I must point out that he has also got faults. He walks in, instead of gliding in on the balls of his feet, and he could get knocked cold with a left hook as he comes in. Bruno has tons of potential but he must be brought along slowly and not rushed.' I noted what Mr Dundee had to say because I respect all that he has achieved as a trainer, but I still feel that I can get much more power into my punches if I have my leading foot firmly on the canvas rather than with the heel off the ground. When I study videos of any of the great punchers in history, like Louis, Liston, Shavers and Dempsey, I notice they always have their feet firmly planted when throwing their knock out shots.

FIGHT No. 18
Opponent: Bill Sharkey (USA)
Venue: Wembley Arena, London
Date: 27 September 1983
WON by knock out, first round

B ILL Sharkey was imported from the United States because it was
considered that he was the sort of ring-wise opponent who could
possibly last the course, and help Frank to get some learning rounds
under his belt. He had gone the distance with a noted puncher in
Mike Weaver, and had held Scott LeDoux to a draw over ten rounds.
So he seemed to have good stamina, as well as a reasonable fight record,
winning twenty-three of his thirty professional contests. But on the
night Sharkey just wasn't big enough for the job.

I was surprised to find Sharkey so small. At thirteen stone eleven
pounds he was having to concede nearly two stone to me and I had a
considerable advantage in height and reach. I knew I needed
experience against opponents of all shapes and sizes, but he didn't
look much bigger than a light-heavyweight. He came charging towards
me at the first bell as if he really meant business. His head was down
and he was swinging punches from all angles. I stood my ground in
the centre of the ring and kept spearing down at him with my left.
The way he was ducking his head made him an inviting target for an
uppercut. I picked my moment to let it go and brought the punch up
from my knees as he rushed blindly forward. The knuckle part of my
glove connected with the point of his chin, and he collapsed face first
to the canvas, leaving referee Roland Dakin with the job of counting
to ten.

I still didn't know how I would cope if any of my fights went the
distance. Sharkey told the press later: 'I've been in the ring with George
Foreman, and Bruno's punching power is comparable to his.' It was
good to have my name mentioned in the same breath as an all-time
great like George Foreman, but the media were still not completely
sold on me. There was still a feeling around that I was being fed easy
opponents. I didn't pick them. All I could do was try to beat them in
as positive a way as possible.

FIGHT No. 19
Opponent: Floyd Cummings (USA)
Venue: Royal Albert Hall, London
Date: 11 October 1983
WON by stoppage, seventh round

IF you've ever been kicked by an elephant you might have a rough idea how Frank felt at the end of the first round of his fight against Floyd Cummings. I say an elephant because Cummings was nicknamed 'Jumbo', having the powerful build of a bull elephant. Before Frank tells you about the fight let me tell you about the man.

At the age of seventeen, Cummings had been sentenced to a fifty-to-seventy-five year jail sentence after being found guilty along with three others of the shooting of a grocer during a robbery in January 1967, when one Franklyn Bruno was six years old and running pretty wild in the backstreets of Wandsworth. Being locked up was nothing new for Cummings. He was arrested for the first time when he was eight. His grandmother, who was bringing him up, told the police she couldn't handle him and he was sent to what he described as a kids' prison in Mississippi.

It was in Stateville Maximum Security Prison that Cummings first got hooked on boxing. He started off concentrating on weightlifting – which explains his stunning physique – and then switched to boxing after being discouraged to find that the top weights he could pump were way below the world records being set by Russian lifters. A top amateur boxer called Billy 'Boy' Thompson arrived at the prison and Cummings was talked into taking him on. Thompson was the 1970 Golden Gloves heavyweight champion and had beaten Ron Lyle and floored George Foreman. Cummings beat Thompson twice in behind-prison-walls amateur contests and it was then he decided that boxing was going to be his sport.

Cummings was released on parole after serving twelve years of his sentence and, aged twenty-nine, he immediately turned professional. He won his first fourteen fights before being outpointed by an outstanding prospect called Renaldo Snipes, who complained after the fight that Cummings had bitten him on the shoulder. In his seventeenth contest he held former world champion 'Smokin'' Joe

Frazier to a draw. He then suffered four successive defeats against Larry Frazier, Mitchell Green, Tim Witherspoon and Jeff Sims. It was then that he was matched with Bruno and everybody was agreed it would be easily his toughest hurdle to date. But nobody guessed quite how tough it would be.

The fight was televised live by the BBC and I can give a clear account of the first round because I have watched the replay dozens of times. I kept Cummings on the end of my jab for most of the round. He was concentrating on trying to slip inside my lead and to throw clubbing punches to my head. But I could see them coming and was able to block them or step out of range. The round was into its last minute when Cummings drove me to the ropes. I threw a left hook counter which he managed to duck. He had his head down and I, amateurishly I have to admit, was standing too stiff and erect, with my head held high and my chin sticking out as if to dry. Crouching in front of me, Cummings suddenly threw an over-the-top right that caught me flush on the jaw. I can only describe this clearly because of the television replays. To be honest, at the time I didn't know what had hit me. It was as if I had suddenly been given an electric shock. I was out on my feet but, thank God, the bell rang before he could throw a follow-up punch that would almost certainly have knocked me over for the first time in my career.

As referee Mike Jacobs caught hold of me Terry Lawless appeared at my side as if he had come up through a trap-door in the ring. I think he must have set some sort of world record for getting through the ropes and into the ring. He steered me back to the corner where he, along with Jimmy Tibbs and Frank Black, worked overtime to bring me round. My senses were coming back and when Terry asked me how many fingers he was holding up I was able to tell him 'two'. As I prepared to go out for the second round my head was still spinning but I was able to digest Terry's clear instructions: 'Keep that jab pumping out and your chin tucked in to your shoulder. Don't let him get on top of you. And don't get caught on the ropes.'

The second round was one of the toughest I have ever known, and I had to reach down deep into my heart to make myself get through it. 'You're not going to let this man beat you' I kept saying to myself as

I bit hard on my gumshield and tried to avoid the big bombs that were coming my way. Cummings was throwing everything at me. I tried to keep him off with my jab, but my timing and rhythm were out of sync. I just couldn't get it together and he hit me with at least six good, clean shots during that nightmare three minutes.

When I returned to the corner, Jimmy Tibbs greeted me with the words: 'You're going to win this, Frank. The feller's punched himself out.' He could have fooled me, but Terry added: 'It's true, Frank. He's hit you with his best shots and it's broken his heart that you're still standing. He's puffing and panting like an old man. Now you can begin to take charge. Shorten your punches and you'll find him easy to hit.'

I did as I was told and started to throw short jabs and hooks that thudded through the defence of Cummings. My confidence came back as I realised a lot of the sting had gone out of his punches, and by the fourth round it was Cummings who was beginning to rock on his heels as I unloaded some of my heaviest ammunition. He was getting so desperate by the fifth round that he started introducing rough house tactics, holding my arms in a vice-like grip every time he got to close quarters. Twice he tried deliberately to butt me, and referee Mike Jacobs gave him a stern warning. I could feel the strength draining out of him in the sixth round – the farthest I had been taken as a professional – and every time we went into a clinch he was breathing so heavily that he sounded like an old steam engine.

I had got myself right back into the fight, and early in the seventh round I twice measured him with my left before throwing follow through rights that made him stagger. He left himself wide open, and I put everything into a right hook that caught him on the side of the jaw and sent him sprawling to the canvas. He pulled himself up at seven but then immediately went down again on one knee and the referee signalled that it was all over. I had passed my toughest test.

It was suggested that the way I reacted when Cummings landed his right hand punch in the first round proved I couldn't take a punch. What rubbish! I know that most people would have been flattened. It was a real cracker and the fact that I was able to recover from it and go on and win satisfied those in the know that I *could* take a punch.

135

FIGHT No. 20
Opponent: Walter Santemore (USA)
Venue: Royal Albert Hall, London
Date: 6 December 1983
WON by knock out, fourth round

THE public reaction to Frank's recovery against 'Jumbo' Cummings was astonishing. He received hundreds of letters congratulating him on the way he had fought back. That fight more than any other cemented his special place in the hearts of the general public. But Frank was far from happy with his performance, and was determined not to give Walter Santemore a glimpse of his chin in his next fight. Santemore was not a noted big puncher, but the fact that he had outpointed one of the modern greats in Earnie Shavers was a warning that he had to be taken seriously. He was a former policeman from New Orleans who knew every trick in the book and some that have never been published. There were a lot of defeats on his long record, but only by some of the finest heavyweights around, top-class fighters of the calibre of John Tate, James 'Quick' Tillis, Jeff Sims and 'Bonecrusher' Smith. Thirty-two-year-old Santemore looked to be the ideal type of opponent for Frank to face following his scare against Cummings.

I couldn't wait to get back into the ring after the fight with Cummings. I knew how close I had come to defeat, and wanted to prove to everybody, most of all to myself, that it had just been a one-off fright. From what I had learned about Santemore, he would be a cagey opponent who had the ability to mess me about. He had mixed with good opponents, and I was going to have to be at my best if I was going to silence the doubters after the way Cummings had rocked me in that first round.

At the weigh-in, Santemore, 6 feet 5 inches tall, scaled just over sixteen stone three pounds, which gave him a weight advantage of nearly half a stone. 'Back home I'm known as "Mad Dog",' he told me after stepping off the scales.'Tonight, man, you're gonna find out just why.' But I reckoned he was more of an old fox than a mad dog and I refused to fall for his clowning tricks in the first round. He was doing a sort of heavy-footed Ali shuffle that amused the crowd, but I wasn't in the ring for a laugh. All the time he was pretending to clown he was looking for the chance to throw the sort of right hands that he had seen land from Jumbo Cummings when shown a video of our fight. I was well prepared for them and, with my chin tucked into my shoulder, stabbed him off with my left jab. As he returned to his corner at the end of this opening round Santemore had blood seeping from a cut under his left eye.

There was less dancing and more punching from Santemore in the second round. He tried to rough me up inside and caught me high on the head with a couple of sneaky rights, and then put everything into a right uppercut. Santemore spun off balance as the punch missed its intended target. I was now on red alert and tossed my first big right of the night. It landed too high to do any real damage but carried enough force to send Santemore back into a neutral corner. I tried to follow up, but he showed what a cunning old so-and-so he was by tieing me up and rolling and smothering as I tried to pin him on the ropes.

Santemore, damaged around his left eye, knew his time was running out and came gunning for me in the third round. He forced me on the retreat with a volley of swinging lefts and rights which were falling short. He then went back to his clowning tactics, winding his right up like a baseball pitcher and then throwing the left. All the time this was going on I was waiting patiently for the chance to get in with a really telling right. The opening came in the last seconds of the round, and I clipped him on the jaw with a short, chopping right hook. He went over on his side but was up almost straight away as the bell rang. As I returned to my corner I knew that I would soon have the 'Mad Dog' muzzled.

Showman Santemore tried to kid me into thinking I was not worrying him by starting the fourth round with a sort of clumsy tap dance. But I quickly had him doing a break dance on the canvas. I measured him with a left lead, and then put all my body-weight behind a follow-through right that landed high on the side of Santemore's left cheek. He crashed on his back and I knew that my night's was work finished. With a great show of courage, Santemore managed to get himself into a standing position at a count of nine, but he was in no position to defend himself and referee Roland Dakin signalled that he had been knocked out.

FIGHT No. 21
Opponent: Juan Figueroa (Argentina)
Venue: Wembley Arena, London
Date: 13 March 1984
WON by knock out, first round

JUAN Figueroa was lined up as Frank's first opponent of 1984. The reporters punching their typewriter keys dismissed him as a push-over, but it was Bruno who had to do the real punching and he was determined to treat him with full respect. Figueroa was the thirty-year-old heavyweight champion of Argentina, stood six-and-a-half feet tall and weighed in at just three-and-a-half pounds under fifteen stone. He worked in his family's market gardening business and was nicknamed the 'Giant of the Market'. Figueroa had been a professional since 1976 and while his record was punctuated with several defeats there was also evidence that he could hurt when he hit. He had stopped fourteen opponents on his way to twenty victories.

All those people who had counted out Figueroa before a punch had been thrown were no doubt claiming they had been proved right when I won the fight in just sixty-seven seconds. But in fairness to Figueroa I should stress that it was two good, solid punches to the jaw that put him over and out. I measured him with a left jab, and then I let go with my favourite left hook, right cross combination. Figueroa folded in front of me, and I knew from the moment of my double connection that he had lost all interest in the fight as referee Harry Gibbs went through the formality of counting him out while I stood in a neutral corner willing him to get up.

It was frustrating for me because I was looking for a much longer fight. I wanted to try out all the new punch patterns that I had been learning in the three months since my last fight. I was now bursting to be tested by somebody who was really well established on the heavyweight scene. Terry Lawless agreed that my apprenticeship was over and 'live' American television was arranged for my next fight to give me vital exposure in the United States. Out of the opposite corner would be coming a fighter called James 'Bonecrusher' Smith.

FIGHT No. 22
Opponent: James 'Bonecrusher' Smith (USA)
Venue: Wembley Arena, London
Date: 13 May 1984
LOST by knock out, round ten

IT was while he was serving in the United States Army in Germany that James Smith became known as 'Bonecrusher'. On a disastrous Sunday night at Wembley (the unlucky thirteenth) it was Frank's bones that were crushed as 'Bonecrusher' became 'Bruno-crusher', and he was counted out for the first (and only) time in his career.

Smith had never laced on a boxing glove in his life until he was twenty-three. He had concentrated on basketball while at high school and college in his hometown of Magnolia, North Carolina. Sergeant Smith started boxing for his Army base and picked up his nickname after reeling off twenty-five knock out victories in thirty-five amateur contests. After leaving the Army, Smith became a guard at Raleigh Maximum Security Prison and started boxing professionally to help feed his young family. He was not one hundred per cent fit for his debut and was stopped in four rounds after coming in as a late substitute against hot prospect James Broad. Smith was encouraged by his performance because he had given Broad a lot of trouble until, as he put it,'I ran out of steam because I had not trained properly.' He wondered what he could achieve if he got himself into good shape. The answer was thirteen successive victories, and the last nine inside the distance.

His fifteenth professional fight was to be back in Europe where he had first started boxing. And waiting to face 29-year-old Smith in a ten-round international contest was one Frank Bruno.

The night started disastrously for Terry Lawless's EastEnders stable. Mark Kaylor, British middleweight champion, was knocked down five times before being stopped in the seventh round by Philadelphian power puncher Buster Drayton. It was a shock defeat that torpedoed his world title hopes, and it dropped a heavy cloud of gloom on the dressing-room. This was hardly the best atmosphere to prepare Bruno for his battle with 'Bonecrusher'.

NBC of America were showing the fight live on their coast-to-coast sports programme and I knew a good performance against Smith would increase my earning potential by at least another 'nought'. He was equally keen to do well because he was already being mentioned as a possible world title contender.

Smith was an inch taller than me, well muscled and, at sixteen stone three pounds, outweighing me by five-and-a-half pounds. I won't bore you with a long breakdown of the fight. To be honest, it was never a classic. Perhaps there was too much at stake for both of us. I never really got into any rhythm but managed to dictate most of the rounds with a left jab that was rarely out of Smith's face. He fought crudely at times, but was always threatening danger with looping rights that travelled in a similar arc to the punch with which 'Jumbo' Cummings caused me problems.

We had both used up a lot of energy by the time the fight was into the eighth round, which was unknown territory for me. Smith's right eye was swollen and he was looking the worse for wear, but for the first time in my professional career I was feeling tired to the point of exhaustion. It wasn't Smith's punches that had got to me. He had hardly hurt me at all. It was the tension. The occasion. It had drained me of my usual strength. These are not excuses I'm making. I just want you to realise how a fighter feels when he's up there in the ring and so much is at stake. You feel as if you are not only fighting for yourself but for everybody else in the place, and you don't want to let them down.

In the interval before the last round Terry Lawless told me: 'Don't get involved. He knows he has got to knock you out to win. Just keep that jab pumping into his face. You've got the fight won. Don't do anything silly. Box.' I did not follow the advice. Even though I was winning the fight by a mile, I knew I hadn't impressed anybody – the Wembley fans or the American television viewers – and I decided I would give them something to remember me by. Well, I certainly did that, but not in the way I intended. I went out for that final round with one thought in mind – to knock 'Bonecrusher's' block off. But he had his own script in mind. As I went hunting him with a big right he swung a left hook to the side of my jaw that knocked me back onto the ropes. Suddenly I felt as if I had fallen down a deep, black hole. If I

140

had been more experienced I would – and should – have gone down for a count while my head cleared. But a mixture of inexperience and stupid pride made me try to stay upright as Smith pounded me with fourteen punches. I promise you I didn't count them at the time. I've watched action replays of the fight so many times that every blow is cemented into my memory. When I watch the video of the fight it is as if I am looking at somebody else trapped on the ropes. I used to force myself to watch it so that I could learn from the situation. My critics jumped in with the view that Bonecrusher had proved in that final round that I had a weak chin. I took no notice of them because I knew that if my chin had been weak that first left hook would have knocked me down and out. The fourteen punches that followed from one of the biggest punchers in the heavyweight division would have knocked over a horse.

Finally I fell sideways to the canvas. I had watched Harry Gibbs count out several of my opponents, including Juan Figueroa in my last contest. Now he was a blurred figure counting over me. I could hear his voice shouting out the count but it seemed to be coming from the end of a tunnel. All my instincts were urging me to drag myself up, but my limbs no longer seemed to belong to me. I've seen on the video how I tried to pull myself back up by holding on to the ropes, but I had lost all sense of direction. By the time I had focused sufficiently to realise exactly where I was and what was happening it was too late, and Harry Gibbs was shouting: '...eight...nine...out!'

That final volley of punches from Smith had opened a gash inside my mouth which needed eight stitches. But I found that I could handle the physical pain. It was how I reacted to the mental pain that would be the big test. Once the disappointment of defeat had worn off I was not as low as some people expected. The defeat helped me grow up almost overnight and make a man of me. I had dished out plenty of punishment against my previous opponents, and now I knew what it was like to be on the receiving end. At least I was free of the pressure of carrying round the 'unbeaten' tag that gets heavier after every fight. I looked for all the positive vibes I could find, and I can now look back and say that the knock out by Bonecrusher did me a favour. It just made me all the more determined to prove myself. Bonecrusher had crushed my bones but not my spirit.

FIGHT No. 23
Opponent: Ken Lakusta (Canada)
Venue: Wembley Arena, London
Date: 25 September 1984
WON by knock out, second round

E VEN Frank's severest critics had to admit he had chosen a tough road back when it was announced that he had been matched with Canadian Ken Lakusta in a ten-round eliminator for the Commonwealth heavyweight title. In the four months since the Bonecrusher disaster he had worked hard at convincing himself that the defeat was the best thing that could have happened to him. This is when he started really believing in the power of positive thinking, and he was ready to take his new attitude into the ring against a noted iron man.

For the first time in my career I weighed in at more than sixteen stone – one-and-a-half pounds over to be exact, which gave me a full stone advantage over the rugged Canadian, who had given Trevor Berbick a tough time for ten rounds in a Commonwealth title fight just a year earlier.

Following my Bonecrusher defeat, Lakusta obviously thought he was going to catch me low on confidence and resistance. He came rushing at me in the opening seconds like a wild bull, but I pulled him up in his tracks with a series of short hooks and uppercuts. When he landed with a long, swinging right he was shocked to find me responding with a left hook-right cross combination that forced him to hold on to me like a drowning man at sea. There was a hint of desperation in Lakusta's work at the start of the second round. He was crowding me and throwing wild punches that suggested he wanted to get things over and done with as quickly as possible. I gave him his wish. After stabbing him off with jarring straight lefts I picked my spot for what I had nicknamed my 'nuclear' right – a long hook-cum-cross that crashed on to the side of his jaw. He dropped in a neutral corner where referee John Coyle counted him out. I instinctively dropped to my knees in a gesture of thanks to God. The Bonecrusher defeat was out of my system already. Bruno – the new Bruno – was back in business.

142

FIGHT No. 24
Opponent: Jeff Jordan (USA)
Venue: Royal Albert Hall, London
Date: 6 November 1984
WON by stoppage, third round

IF Jeff Jordan, from the Jack Nicklaus city of Columbus, Ohio, had fought as good a fight as he talked he would have been one of the all-time great heavyweights. He was completely dismissive of Frank before their top-of-the-bill battle at the Royal Albert Hall, but provided little action to go with his brave words. He had won seventeen of his twenty fights since turning professional six months before Bruno, but his mediocre performance suggested that there must be seventeen novice heavyweights out there.

My fight plan was to keep the stocky Jordan on the end of my left jab until I had seen what he had to offer. For the first minute I hardly had my left glove out of his face. He was threatening all sorts of things with swinging counter punches that were falling well short. As I forced him back towards his corner, one of his seconds shouted: 'Come on, Jeff Baby, let's get acquainted.' Jeff Baby's face was beginning to redden, but he didn't seem in the slightest bit concerned. 'You ain't got nothin', sucker,' he told me as we went into a clinch. My reply was to unload four heavy rights that all landed on target and brought up a nasty swelling under his left eye. Goodness knows what was going on in Jordan's corner, but I was told afterwards that the final instruction from his second as he came out for round two was: 'If he tags you, run like hell.'

I caught him with an uppercut that made him buckle at the knees. But he didn't run like hell. Instead he grabbed me in a sort of grizzly bear hold. 'Is that the best you can do, sucker?' he said. He kept on talking and I kept on punching until referee Sid Nathan decided that he had taken enough punishment after a right hook had opened a gash over his left eye in round three. As my arm was raised, the defiant Jordan said: 'You couldn't knock me down, sucker'. But as I looked at his bruised, bloody face I knew who the real sucker was.

FIGHT No. 25
Opponent: Phil Brown (USA)
Venue: Wembley Arena, London
Date: 27 November 1984
WON on points, 10 rounds

FRANK at last found out what it is like to hear a final bell, but it was not music to his ears. He was taken the distance for the first time in his career by Phil Brown, an opponent who came to Wembley only to survive. Brown had been beaten only once since leaving the penitentiary back home in New Orleans where boxing had saved him from a downhill run to a life on the wrong side of the law. He had a respectable ring record, winning twenty-two fights and drawing two. The fact that he had outpointed the once highly rated Jimmy Young was proof that he was a capable fighter. His undefeated record had been wrecked in his last fight when he was stopped in the fourth round by former world title contender Gerry Cooney, who was making a comeback in the unlikely place of Anchorage, Alaska.

Phil Brown gave me just about the most frustrating night of my life. I got a lot of stick from the critics, but I don't think they took into account the fact that it's really difficult to perform well against an opponent who is thinking only of stopping you from getting into any sort of rhythm. He smothered and covered, twisted and turned, ducked and dived and clutched and grabbed. Brown did just about everything but fight. At six feet three inches and fifteen stone five pounds he must have had a lot of power, but from the first bell all he was concerned with was taking avoiding action. He fought on the retreat and every time I tried to open up he would suddenly trap my gloves by holding, or twist like an eel so that I became tangled up in his arms as I missed with attempted punches. I was doing my best to make it a fight, but Brown just wasn't interested. I had him in real trouble only a couple of times throughout the fight. His defensive, spoiling tactics had drawn all the sting from me. The referee scored it 100 points to me and 95 to Brown, which meant I had won every round. But I was anything but satisfied with my performance.

FIGHT No. 26
Opponent: Lucien Rodriguez (France)
Venue: Wembley Arena, London
Date: 27 March 1985
WON by stoppage, first round

TWO years less one day before this fight Lucien Rodriguez had challenged Larry Holmes for the world heavyweight championship, and he had given an excellent account of himself before losing on points. He had twice won the European title and had made six successful defences, including a points win over British champion David Pearce. In short, Casablanca-born Rodriguez looked capable of giving Frank a tough fight. It was a vital contest for Frank because he was one step away from challenging Anders Eklund for his European championship.

The title fight had been signed up and this put extra pressure on me because I knew I daren't slip up against Rodriguez. I could not miss the gigantic Eklund, who was sitting at the Wembley ringside on a spying mission. I was determined to produce a performance that would cost him sleepless nights. I trained for speed as well as power because I thought I might have to do some chasing before I could catch up with the Frenchman, who liked to try to be a slippery, elusive target. At the weigh-in I scaled a few ounces over fifteen stone twelve pounds, and had a weight advantage of nearly a stone.

The fight started as I expected with Rodriguez 'getting on his bike' and circling backwards around the ring behind a light, flicking left. I was content to follow him for the opening two minutes, watching warily for any sneaky rights while I kept thudding my left into his face. He made the mistake of backing away to the ropes and was unable to retreat any further as I let go with my first serious rights of the fight. I made him sag into the ropes with a right uppercut and followed with a solid right hook. It seemed to take several seconds for the power of the shots to take effect. Suddenly he bowed forward and slowly sank to the canvas as I threw a right left-right combination to the head. Rodriguez rose with great reluctance at the count of nine, and as I stepped forward he shook his head and waved a fist in surrender.

145

FIGHT No. 27
Opponent: Anders Eklund (Sweden)
Venue: Wembley Arena, London
Date: 1 October 1985
WON by knock out, round four

THERE were times when it looked as if Frank would be more likely to meet Anders Eklund in the high court than the ring. First of all they were due to fight in April 1985. This was called off when Eklund claimed he had damaged his hand. Promoters Mike Barrett and Mickey Duff won the purse bidding for the fight with an offer over £200,000. They rescheduled the fight for Wembley on 25 June, but this was postponed following a bitter dispute over television fees with Eklund's manager, Mogens Palle. The fight was finally arranged for Wembley in the autumn, which meant that by the time Frank climbed into the ring he had gone eleven months with less than a round of action. The threat of more legal activity was lifted when Terry Lawless settled out of court on the eve of the fight, paying around £100,000 to at last end the dispute with Burt McCarthy over the piece of paper that Frank had signed with him while still an amateur. Now Frank could concentrate on the most important fight of his life to date.

Thanks to the frustrating postponements, I found it easy to motivate myself for the fight by making Eklund the target for my anger. And the fact that he was walking off with the lion's share of the purse (more than £120,000) further helped put me in the mood to beat him. It was just as well that I had a reason to be annoyed with 27-year-old Eklund because, to be honest, it would have been very easy to have really liked the man. He was a gentle giant outside the ring, quiet spoken and very polite and intelligent. All his fighting had to be done outside his homeland of Sweden where professional boxing was banned.

He was certainly the biggest opponent I have ever met. In fact I doubt if there have been many bigger champions in the history of boxing. He stood a fraction over 6 feet 6 inches tall and usually weighed in at just under seventeen stone. But he had seen what my power punching had done to Lucien Rodriguez, and decided that he would

146

Above: Frank plays it for laughs in a Freddie Starr television special. It was Freddie who helped set Frank up for the This is Your Life surprise.

Right: The late Roy Castle was a good friend of Frank's and helped teach him balance through dancing

By Royal appointment: Frank (above) receives an award for his charity work from the Duke of Edinburgh, and chats with Princess Diana (below). Frank is an official ambassador for the Prince's Trust.

Who's the greatest? Frank meets Lady Thatcher (above) who told him to keep flying the flag for Britain. One of Frank's favourite photographs (below), taken with Muhammad Ali during an early trip to the USA.

Nicola and Laura were in the ring (above) to help Frank celebrate his world title triumph over Oliver McCall, and Rachel (right) was waiting at home to give her Dad a hero's welcome.

Two belting pictures of the WBC heavyweight champion of the world.

One man and his trainer: Frank with George Francis,

Something worth fighting for: It was the arrival of Franklin Junior (above) in March 1995 that gave Frank the extra incentive to take the world title from Oliver McCall (below). As we can see, Franklin Junior is already a hungry biter.

The end of the dream is near as Mike Tyson hammers home a right during their final showdown in Las Vegas.

have a better chance of standing up to my punches if he increased his body bulk. He weighed in for our fight at a mammoth seventeen stone six-and-a-half pounds. I came in at just half a pound over sixteen stone.

I was able to get a good look at Eklund when he won the European championship with a very impressive fourth round stoppage of the previously unbeaten Norwegian Steffen Tangstad. Their title fight was staged in Copenhagen in March 1985, and I was invited to watch it 'live' in the ITV sports studio in London. Eklund destroyed Tangstad with some dynamite punches that showed he had completely recovered from a startling first round defeat by Liverpudlian Noel Quarless and a points set-back against old Joe Bugner.

I made careful note that Eklund strongly favoured his right which he threw in a similar straight-over-the-top style to Ingemar Johansson, the last Swedish heavyweight to dominate Europe some twenty-five years earlier. Johansson had also briefly ruled the world when his 'Ingo's Bingo' landed on the suspect chin of Floyd Patterson. Now Eklund was talking in terms of a world title fight once he had removed me from his path. Sadly for him, I had ambitious plans of my own.

A big worry was removed for me on the eve of my first challenge for a professional championship. I had been scheduled to appear in the high court the morning after the fight to settle the long-running dispute over the piece of paper I had signed with Burt McCarthy four years earlier. Terry knew it was weighing on my mind, and he instructed that the case be settled out of court. It meant I climbed into the Wembley ring in a perfect frame of mind.

As Eklund had come in so heavy for our fight I deliberately set a fast pace right from the first bell. They used to call Primo Carnera the Ambling Alp, and it was a nickname that would have suited Eklund. It was like having a mountain wall in front of you. There was a lot of the champion to hit and from the opening moments I was scoring with stiff left jabs to the head that had him blinking. He seemed a little apprehensive every time I shaped to throw a right, but I was foxing him. I had no intention of letting my big bombs go until I knew I had made a proper opening. Eklund threw few punches in this opening round, but he managed to pierce my defence with a right to the body that made me remember to keep my elbows tucked in. My rat-a-tat-tat jabs brought blood trickling from his nose in the second round and this stirred him into his first big attack. He threw a flurry of long lefts and rights, but I was easily able to smother his punches with the tighter defence that I had been perfecting during the long build-up to the fight. Two big rights did get through to my head just before the bell, but they travelled too far to cause any damage. I returned to my corner confident that I was Eklund's 'guv'nor'. He was beginning to puff because of all the weight he was carrying, and I knew that I had not even got properly warmed up yet. 'It's time to let him feel your right hand,' Terry Lawless said. 'But don't take any chances because he's dangerous with his right. Keep your chin tucked in and let your right go over his left lead.'

For the first minute of the round I gave Eklund no hint of my intentions. I kept the pattern as in the previous two rounds, jabbing and throwing the occasional left hook. Then I let go with my first serious right, a long follow-through after a left lead. It caught Eklund high on the head and I knew it had hurt him when he hung on while his head cleared. The referee pulled us apart and I immediately threw two more quick rights and as they connected with the side of Eklund's head his long legs started to buckle. He had the sense to clutch hold of me and I banged in a left right combination that I felt would have floored him if he had not been so close to me and able to use me as a prop.

I couldn't wait for the fourth round to start. 'Now be careful,' Terry said, seeing the look of clear intent in my eyes. 'You've got him, but he is going to be trying a desperate right. Watch out for it.' But I didn't give Eklund the chance. I almost ran to the centre of the ring and met him with a right over the top of his left lead that had him buckling at the knees. As his head came down towards me I jolted him with a right uppercut, and then followed with two very deliberate over-the-top rights that landed on the side of his massive jaw. They were four of the hardest and most accurate right hand punches I had ever thrown, and the effect on Eklund was dramatic. He pitched forward to the canvas like a giant tree being felled, and squatted dazed and confused in the centre of the ring with blood seeping from a cut over his left eye as Swiss referee Franz Marti counted him out. It was the greatest moment of my career so far. I was the European champion and well on the way to my dream fight for the world heavyweight championship.

FIGHT No. 28
Opponent: Larry Frazier (USA)
Venue: Royal Albert Hall, London
Date: 4 December 1985
WON by knock out, second round

FRANK was keyed up for a challenging battle against highly regarded American Larry Alexander when, just three days before their scheduled fight, he failed the British Boxing Board of Control's strict medical check after a brain scan had revealed an irregularity. Larry Frazier, a 36-year-old Californian, was hastily brought in as a substitute. Frank got really nervous about this sudden change.

I was on a hiding to nothing against Frazier. If I beat him, everybody would say: 'So what, he's an old man who should never have been in the ring with Bruno in the first place.' If I were to lose it would have destroyed my chances of a world title shot when I was within punching distance of the fight I have always dreamed about. I managed to push all negative thoughts out of my head once I was in the ring, and looked on Frazier as the man standing between me and my dream. I was determined to knock him out of my path.

I was at my heaviest ever for the fight at a few ounces over sixteen stone three pounds, but I was still having to give nine pounds to the heftily-built, 6 feet 4 inches tall American. His wide stomach looked an inviting target and I planted several short hooks into it during a first round in which Frazier provided little evidence that he carried the knock out power that he had been boasting about before the fight. The thought that he could shatter my world title dreams with just one punch was uppermost in my mind as I came out for the second round, and I had made up my mind to quickly get it over and done with. I forced him back to the ropes with a series of left jabs and then buried two short, ripping left hooks into the side of his stomach. Frazier grunted as the punches sank in and he fell to the canvas and rolled over in agony. He was clasping his gloves to his stomach as referee Roland Dakin counted him out. All my concentration was now on my next fight – an official eliminator for the world heavyweight title.

FIGHT No. 29
Opponent: Gerrie Coetzee (South Africa)
Venue: Wembley Arena, London
Date: 4 March 1986
WON by stoppage, first round

A WHITE South African with a 'bionic' right hand was now all that stood between Frank and his dream of challenging for the heavy-weight championship of the world, the greatest prize in sport. I mention that he was white only because so many other people had made an issue of it. You will no doubt have noticed that throughout this book Frank has made little reference to the colour or creed of his opponents. Never in his life has he been one for judging people by the shade of their skin. He always takes people as he finds them. The Anti-Apartheid Movement, in these days before the Nelson Mandela-led revolution, tried to put pressure on him not to go ahead with the fight with Gerrie Coetzee. Terry Lawless protected him as much as he could from the campaign aimed at Bruno and the promotion. But the message got through that there were fanatical people who considered him some sort of a traitor for going through with the world title eliminator.

John Conteh, former world light heavyweight champion and an old hero of Frank's, contacted him by letter, putting the Anti-Apartheid Movement's case and asking him to consider pulling out of the fight rather than go into the ring with a white South African who had grown up under Apartheid laws. Frank was not, and never will be, a political animal, but he had every sympathy with the case of the suppressed black people of South Africa. If he had thought not going ahead with the fight might have made any difference to their struggle for equality then he would have seriously considered refusing to fight. But he knew in his heart that it would not have made the tiniest bit of difference.

A withdrawal by me as a token protest would have made front page headlines for a day or two and within a week would have been forgotten. 'Frank Who?' they would have said. There would have been no winners if I had pulled out of the fight, and I would have been a big, big loser. I had fought my heart out to get this far in my career and there was no way I wanted to miss out on the chance of a lifetime. In effect, what the protesters would have achieved had they managed in their attempts to get the promotion cancelled was punish me because of the colour of my skin. Another point I took into consideration was that Coetzee himself was on record as being against Apartheid. He had dozens of black friends and his black sparring partner, Randy Stephens, was best man at his wedding. One more thing – I owed it to my family to go through with the contest. I am a professional sportsman and it is only through boxing that I can give Laura and our family security for life.

I shut the ban-the-fight argument out of my mind and got down to the serious business of training for the fight of my life. Coetzee was past the peak of his career, but he remained one of the most feared punchers in the game. He was known as 'The Bionic Man' because the right fist with which he destroyed so many opponents had been operated on several times, and it was reported that the fist had been strengthened by the insertion of a steel pin. In thirty-five professional fights, Coetzee had been beaten just four times and only by top-flight opposition. John Tate had outpointed him over fifteen rounds in a WBA title fight in 1979, and big-hitting Mike Weaver had stopped him in the thirteenth round of a championship contest in 1980.

In 1981 he lost on points to Renaldo Snipes, and in a 1984 WBA title defence he had been knocked out by Greg Page during a controversial eighth round that had been allowed to run over time. The greatest moment of his career so far had been a tenth round knockout victory over Mike Dokes that clinched the WBA version of the world heavyweight championship in 1983. He had also bombed out Leon Spinks and his countryman Kallie Knoetze, both in the first round, and he had held WBC heavyweight champion Pinklon Thomas to a draw.

In his last fight before facing me he had scored an excellent points victory over a top American prospect, James 'Quick' Tillis. There was criticism of him when he arrived in England accompanied by his wife and children. 'He seems to think he's over here on holiday,' was the sort of thing being said. But I believed Coetzee when he said that he felt more comfortable when his family was with him, and that it helped rather than hindered his concentration.

He seemed almost chillingly confident at one of the pre-fight press conferences. 'Somebody's been lying to Frank,' he said. 'They've been filling his head with stories about me being involved in wars and that I'm not the fighter I was. He has been told that I am an easy short cut to the title. If the people telling him these things truly believe it then they have made the mistake of a lifetime. If he beats me then he will be the next world champ. But that's not going to happen.'

I made the boxing reporters chuckle when I said: 'I am two hundred per cent confident that I will knock him out.' And I really honestly believed it. There was no way in this world that I was going to let him beat me. At the weigh-in I scaled sixteen stone three pounds, which was six-and-a-quarter pounds lighter than the thirty-year-old South African, who was the same height as me. He repeated at the weigh-in that the people who had said he was 'over the top' were telling me lies. In actual fact, Terry Lawless had been telling me the exact opposite. 'You've got to treat him with great respect,' he said. 'He is second only to Earnie Shavers as the biggest puncher of the last fifteen years.'

Coetzee tried the old Muhammad Ali trick of staring me down as we got our last-minute instructions from the referee in the centre of the ring, but I held his stare until he dropped his gaze. I had won the eyeball-to-eyeball confrontation. Now it was time for the real stuff. In our pre-fight planning, it was decided that I should try to get a big punch in as early as possible to test Coetzee's chin and his confidence. I would usually have gone out jabbing for the first couple of minutes before throwing any 'nuclear' punches, but I wanted Coetzee to know as quickly as possible that I carried a dig to match his famous 'bionic' right. While doing our homework on him we noticed that every time he threw a left jab his head came up. My plan was to throw a right counter the moment he jabbed. In the opening minute I backed him up to the ropes with a succession of left leads and then, just as he jabbed with his left, his head came up and I launched my right with a full follow-through of my right shoulder. The knuckle part of my glove connected with his left cheekbone, and Coetzee sat down as if somebody had suddenly pulled a chair from under him. He was up quickly at three, and as he stood taking the mandatory eight count blood started to run down from a cut where my punch had landed. I could see by the glazed look in his eyes that I had hurt him more than he was letting on. I decided then and there to go all out for a quick finish.

As Canadian referee Guy Jutras waved me back into the fight I met Coetzee with full-power left jabs. He tried to grab my arms and pull me to him, but I pushed him off and drove him back across the ring towards his own corner. I was so keen to get to him while he was still dazed that I tried too hard and missed with two over-the-top rights. Coetzee retreated to the far side of the ring and shaped as if he was about to try his first attack of the fight, but before he could let his punches go I connected with a wicked right cross. The punch hit him on the side of the jaw and snapped his head sideways. He collapsed back across the bottom rope and the force of my punch was so great that half his huge body was hanging over the apron, pinning a cameraman to his seat. It was obvious that the fight was over for the unconscious Coetzee. The referee started to count but the noise of the crowd was so great that I couldn't hear it. And poor Coetzee certainly couldn't because he was out to the world. The referee waved his arms to signal that it was all over, and the MC announced: 'After one minute fifty seconds of the first round the referee has stopped the contest.' Some of the newspapers reported that it was a knock out, but Mr Jutras told me: 'I didn't complete the count because I was worried for Gerrie's safety. Sorry to rob you of a k.o. in the record book, but I know you'll understand.'

We were concerned about Coetzee for several minutes, but he then recovered sufficiently to return to his corner. Later, in his dressing-room, he was sporting enough to tell me: 'Frank, I have been fighting for more than twenty years. Nobody has ever done to me what you did tonight. You were magnificent, and I'm going to tell everybody that you will be the next world champion. Good luck to you. You've got a great career to look forward to. This is only the beginning.' And this was the man they wanted to ban. He didn't see me as black Frank Bruno. He saw me as Frank Bruno, human being. And I saw him as Gerrie Coetzee, human being and great sportsman. Back in my dressing-room it was sheer bedlam. Eamonn Andrews and *This Is Your Life* producer Malcolm Morris pushed their way into the crowded room to congratulate me. Terry made Eamonn, a keen student of boxing, release that famous laugh of his when he called out: 'Not now Eamonn...' I was now the official number one contender for the world heavyweight title.

FIGHT No. 30
Opponent: Tim Witherspoon (USA)
Venue: Wembley Stadium, London
Date: 19 July 1986
LOST by stoppage, eleventh round

IT is fascinating to watch Frank in the dressing-room in the final moments before a major fight. He almost goes into a trance as he locks his mind on to the job facing him. I was allowed into the inner sanctum before his world title challenge against Tim Witherspoon at Wembley Stadium in my role as publicist for a fight in which Frank was attempting to become the first British-born world heavyweight champion since Bob Fitzsimmons (Cornish born, New Zealand raised) in 1897.

Almost exactly ten years earlier I had been on Wembley Stadium dressing-room duty as a football reporter covering England's triumphant 1966 World Cup campaign. The setting was the same, and there was a similar stomach-churning tension in the air. The major difference was that Frank was on his own, while Bobby Moore and his team-mates had each other to help them over the pre-match nerves hurdle.

The tight-knit Bruno team of manager Lawless, coach Jimmy Tibbs and trainer Frank Black had completed their thorough preparation work, and respectfully kept to one side as Frank went through his pre-fight ritual. He sat on a straight-backed chair in the middle of the vast dressing-room, glistening like a thoroughbred racehorse after having had his body smothered in coconut oil to keep his muscles supple. In his hands he held a worn, well-thumbed Bible that had been given to him many years earlier by his mother. Tucked inside the back page was a special prayer that he silently mouthed during the final countdown to the call to leave the dressing-room for his appointment in the ring:

'Dear Lord God, Father Almighty,
I know that with so much want and misery in the world it is selfish and remiss of me to ask for something that is for me alone. But on this one occasion, oh Lord, I ask you to give me the strength, the courage

155

and willpower to become the heavyweight boxing champion of the world. In so doing I would be better able to spread your Word, and give an example of Christian beliefs and attitudes to the young people that I am fortunate enough to have following my lead. More than ever, oh mighty Father, I need you in my corner when I make my challenge for the world title, and I ask you to help make me a winner of whom everybody can be proud. I appreciate and understand that there are many more vital things to concern you, but this is the most important moment of my life, and I pray that you can fill me with the fire and determination that will be needed to win the championship. Win or lose, please let me conduct myself with dignity and grace and make it so that neither I nor my opponent suffer any serious injury. I hope and pray that I get the opportunity to be your spokesman as heavyweight champion of the world, but regardless of the result I will remain your humble and obedient servant. Through Jesus Christ Our Lord, Amen.'

Twenty yards away in the 'Visitors' dressing-room across the concrete corridor that leads uphill to the tradition-soaked Wembley football pitch, Tim Witherspoon was going through his final preparations surrounded by a noisy thirty-strong entourage of trainers, sparring partners, relatives and minders, most of them dressed in matching jazzy tracksuits. Tim had 'been there, done that' and was much more laid-back about the task ahead as the after-midnight fight approached. The high-ceilinged room rocked to the sounds of soul music blaring from a ghetto-blaster, and it seemed more like a disco club than a dressing-room. Wembley had never experienced anything quite like it for a sports occasion.

'Terrible Tim', as he had been nicknamed by Muhammad Ali when he acted as the then champion's young sparring partner, had fought six fewer times than Bruno, but had mixed in much higher company. He had won twenty-four of his twenty-six professional fights, and one of his defeats – a points loss to Larry Holmes in a WBC world title fight in 1983 – had been loudly disputed. He had won the vacant WBC championship in 1984 by outpointing Greg Page, and had then lost it in his first defence against Pinklon Thomas, another of the procession of come-and-go champions who collectively became known as 'The Alphabet Boys'.

In January 1986 Witherspoon captured the WBA version of the world title by outpointing Tony Tubbs, and had returned to the boxing beat after group therapy treatment to help him overcome a drug dependency problem. Now Bruno was praying that he could relieve him of the title.

I felt that I knew Witherspoon almost as well as he knew himself. Ever since I had earned the fight with him by beating Coetzee I had made a special study of him on a collection of videos. I admired and respected him as a boxer who was a fine all-round technician with a clubbing right hand that he liked to swing over the top of an opponent's defence almost in the style of a cricketer bowling a ball. I knew I had to be careful of that punch. He would be seven pounds heavier than me, but – with a reach of 82 inches – I had a five inch reach advantage and I planned to make full use of it by getting behind a long left jab, which I would use as a foundation-builder for the heavier blows to come from my follow-through rights and left hooks.

My fight strategy was to keep nice and tight for the opening rounds and operate behind a solid left jab. It was clear from Witherspoon's record that he had a strong chin and he had never taken a count throughout his amateur and professional career. I knew it would be unwise to launch a nuclear attack in the first round as I had against Coetzee. I needed to conserve my energy for what would almost certainly be a long journey, and I had steeled myself for having to go fifteen rounds for the first time.

For the first five rounds I was in charge of the fight, keeping Tim on the end of my left jab and getting out of clinches as quickly as possible. He was doing his best to turn it into a rough-house fight, but I stuck to my boxing plan because I knew that in a free-for-all I would come off second best. Don't ask me why, but Americans are better brawlers than the Brits. Having been to the States on many occasions and visited the ghettos, I guess the reason is that they have to fight harder in the streets to survive. The mean streets of New York, Los Angeles and Philadelphia make Wandsworth seem about as rough as a school playground.

I didn't manage to hit Witherspoon with my best combinations, but

I landed the sort of single punches that would have blasted out virtually any other heavyweight in the world. Each time Tim just took a step backwards and then closed up on me before I could follow up with the combination punches I had practised for hours on end in the gym. He had an exceptionally strong chin, yet I know that I had him worried several times during the early stages of the fight. Whenever I pinned him with a good punch he would smother and cover and get to close quarters until his head had cleared, and then he would come back with those crude but effective swings of his. He clubs you with his fists and I have to admit that he was a much harder puncher than I had imagined.

The turning point of the fight came midway through the sixth round when I stupidly allowed Witherspoon to kid me into following him to the ropes, and as I went to throw a right he caught me on the side of the jaw with a swinging left and then a clumping right to the side of my head. For the first time I had to seek the safety of a clinch as I waited for the mist to clear from my eyes. Tim's swollen left eye was beginning to close and he had been breathing heavily for the last couple of rounds, but he now knew that he had hurt me and this did wonders for his confidence.

My stamina started to drain away from me, and I could only imagine it was due to all the tension during the build-up to the fight. I felt as if I was just in front going into the tenth round, but the fact that there was still a third of the fight to go was playing on my mind. I got Witherspoon angry with a couple of rights that drifted off target on to the back of his neck and he complained to the referee. I interpreted this as showing that he was beginning to run out of steam himself and as I went out for the eleventh round I decided to unload some heavy ammunition in a bid to get the fight over. I thought I was just getting the better of the round and I remember whacking him with a right cross that would have dropped most heavyweights. At exactly the same moment he caught me with a right of his own on the side of my jaw. From then on everything is hazy in my memory. I can just recall trying desperately to hold on to him while I got my senses back together, and I later saw on video how he started to hurl those cricket bowler's punches at me. Two more clubbing rights sent me reeling across the ring. I remember bashing backwards against Witherspoon's cornerpost and I knew my dream of winning the world title had disappeared as I went down in a daze.

They later told me that Witherspoon had hit me three times while I was down but I was not aware of it. I was lost in a world of mists and mazes as the referee Isidro Rodriguez waved the fight over. Now that I look back I realise that I was not quite ready for the challenge. At twenty-four, my chance had come a year or so too early.

FIGHT No. 31
Opponent: James Tillis (USA)
Venue: Wembley Arena, London
Date: 24 March 1987
WON by stoppage, fifth round

GREG Page, former WBC world heavyweight champion, was lined up as the comeback opponent for Frank's first fight after his defeat by Tim Witherspoon, but he pulled out because of an eye injury. James 'Quick' Tillis, a cowboy from Oklahoma, was called in as a substitute. His main claim to fame was the he had been the first man to take Mike Tyson the distance. He got his 'Quick' nickname because of his fast hands and speedy footwork, and he also had a quick tongue. Tillis, wearing a cowboy hat, told the British press before the fight: 'I've not come here as a stepping stone for Bruno. I'm gonna rustle him, ride him, rope him, brand him and corral him.'

There was a lot riding on the fight because the winner would almost certainly be a future title-fight opponent for Mike Tyson, who watched the contest as a co-commentator alongside my old pal, Harry Carpenter. A lot of people had written me off after the defeat by Witherspoon. With so much to motivate me, I gave poor old Jimmy Tillis quite a going over. I shook off my ring rust and took command of the fight from the first bell, forcing Tillis on to his back foot with two-handed combinations that I had been sharpening under the ll-knowning eye of my new trainer George Francis.

I had just one critical moment in the second round when Tillis landed a cracking right counter to my jaw. I went into a clinch, held on the blind side of the referee Francis-style until my head had cleared and then regained control with a barrage of lefts and rights to the head. Midway through the fifth round Tillis waved a glove in surrender and turned his back on me after solid lefts and rights had ripped gashes on his nose and eyebrow. As referee John Coyle waved the fight over Mike Tyson told BBC-TV viewers: 'I'm very impressed. That's a tremendous job by Frank. Tillis is a durable guy. Frank will be a very good opponent for me, and I look forward to fighting him.'

FIGHT No. 32
Opponent: Chuck Gardner (USA)
Venue: Palais des Festivals, Cannes
Date: 27 June 1987
WON by knock out, first round

THERE was an embarrassingly unforgettable night of French farce for Frank when he was matched in the Palais des Festivals in Cannes against an American called Chuck Gardner. The alarm bells should have rung when American-inspired reports started appearing in the newspapers dismissing Gardner as 'a washed-up bum'. Rival promoter Frank Warren tossed in his two-pennyworth when he claimed: 'My gardener could do better against Bruno than Gardner.' It was all worrying stuff, and with the benefit of hindsight they should have called the whole thing off before Frank was dragged into what was described by one newspaper as 'the biggest boxing scandal for years', and to make matters worse it was all screened 'live' on BBC television.

I have to be honest and say that I could not believe it when I first clapped eyes on Gardner before the fight. He was supposed to have been thirty-three but looked at least ten years older. At seventeen stone four pounds he seemed to be carrying about two stone surplus weight, and most of it was draped around his waist in great rolls of fat. I wondered what the viewers at home would make of him when they watched the fight. Mind you, they did not see him for long. He collapsed as if he had been shot when I connected with the first punch that I threw, a half jab, half hook to the side of the face. It was all over in fifty-nine seconds, most of it spent with me stalking Gardner as he almost galloped backwards around the ring.

Gardner slipped under the bottom rope and lay perfectly still with his head resting on the apron. The referee did not bother to count him out, but bent down to remove his gumshield. As he did so, it looked as if Gardner's set of upper dentures came out at the same time. It was like something out of a *Monty Python* sketch. There was uproar in the press, with the BBC getting much of the flak for screening a fight that provided the most embarrassing evening of my life. My excuse was that I did not pick my opponents. I just fought them.

161

FIGHT No. 33
Opponent: Reggie Gross (USA)
Venue: Marbella, Spain
Date: 20 August 1987
WON by stoppage, eighth round

FRANK wanted to get back into the ring as quickly as possible to try to bury the memory of the Gardner fiasco, and his wish was granted two months later. This time he travelled to the holiday resort of Marbella in Spain where, waiting in the bullring to meet him, there was another American opponent: Reggie Gross, who was substituting for Greg Page, a man Frank seemed destined not to meet in the ring. Gross had been knocked out in the first round by Mike Tyson, but had a reasonable record before then. His career had been brought to an abrupt halt when he was arrested on a charge of murdering a man with a gun. He spent seven months in prison before being cleared of the charge, and now he was looking to re-launch his career – with Bruno as his stepping stone back towards the top.

Our fight was to be the chief supporting contest to the world welterweight championship defence by Lloyd Honeyghan against Texan Gene Hatcher. After a 24-hour delay caused by non-stop rain Lloyd wasted no more time, bombing out Hatcher in just forty-five seconds. I took a lot longer against an opponent who seemed more intent on ducking and diving than fighting. Gross was allowed to stand up to my punches for eight of the scheduled ten rounds before the Spanish referee at last stopped what was one-way traffic to save the man from Baltimore soaking up any more punishment.

It takes two to tango, and the plodding Gross did not seem the slightest bi t interested in doing anything apart from trying to dodge and block my punches. I had been whacking a stream of punches through the defence of Gross without reply, and the referee could have stopped it at least two rounds earlier. I was then lined up for what would be a world title eliminator against Trevor Berbick, but he pulled out with an injury. There was great consolation. In his place I would at long last be fighting Joe Bugner.

FIGHT No. 34
Opponent: Joe Bugner (Australia)
Venue: White Hart Lane, London
Date: 24 October 1987
WON by stoppage, eighth round

ALMOST from the moment that Frank threw his first punch as a professional he was haunted by the name of Joe Bugner. He was just beginning to make a name for himself in the ring when Frank first laced on the gloves as an eight-year-old tearaway schoolboy. In 1971, the year before Frank was sent to Oak Hall, Bugner was adjudged to have outpointed great heavyweight hero Henry Cooper in a triple title fight for the British, European and Commonwealth championships. It was a disputed decision and Hungarian-born Joe, then just twenty-one, was never really forgiven for beating 'Our 'Enery', who bowed out at the age of thirty-seven with the fans still very much on his side.

Eleven years later when Frank launched his professional career, Bugner was in the United States flirting with the third of several comebacks, and ringside reporters were making comparisons between Bugner and Bruno almost from Frank's first fight. By the time Frank had got thirteen wins under his belt Bugner had returned to Britain to resume his comeback and he made no secret of the fact that he had Bruno in his sights.

Despite several attempts to get them together, including a proposed open-air fight in Vienna, the political mountains were always too high to climb. Bugner got fed up hanging around waiting for them to be matched and he emigrated to Australia in 1985. That it seemed was the end of any chance of a Bugner-Bruno showdown.

At about the time that Frank was preparing for his world title challenge against Tim Witherspoon news came through from Down Under that Joe – now 'Aussie Joe' – was getting himself in shape for a fourth comeback campaign. Also round about that time a new face started popping up on the British boxing scene – millionaire snooker entrepreneur Barry Hearn. He was from the same Essex territory as Terry Lawless, and to where Bruno had moved soon after the start of his professional career. Hearn was the supremo of the enormously successful Romford Matchroom Snooker club that had produced a diamond of a player in Steve Davis, and he was largely responsible for turning snooker into a hugely popular television sport. He and near-neighbour Lawless became pals, and when Bruno travelled to Brentwood for a face-to-face meeting with Witherspoon to publicise the fight, it was Barry who drove them there in his Rolls-Royce. It was also noted that he took a seat on the stage for the press conference, drinking in the atmosphere and taking a keen interest in every aspect of the fight.

He later revealed to Lawless that his big ambition was to promote boxing with the same sort of style and flair that he had brought to the world of snooker. They agreed in the summer of 1987 to form an alliance, concentrating at first on small-hall shows where Terry's stable of boxers could get much-needed work and projection. It seemed the new partnership had hardly been going five minutes when Barry started quietly asking Frank's opinion of Joe Bugner.

'Do you think you could beat him?' he asked.

'I've never doubted it,' Bruno said, truthfully.

When he announced that he was going to try to bring Bugner over from Australia to fight Bruno Terry burst out laughing. 'You can forget that one,' he said. 'There's no chance.'

Mickey Duff, who had cut his close ties with Bugner, agreed that it was a waste of time trying to get them together in the ring.

That was just the challenge that Hearn needed. He admits that he likes nothing better than to try to prove the impossible is possible.

Everything seemed to be against him. He was talking about an autumn open-air fight, which would be a gamble with the weather, and he had to get past perhaps the toughest barrier of them all – Joe Bugner's wife, Marlene. Then there was the little matter that Joe faced the threat of arrest if he stepped foot in Britain because of alleged non-payment of alimony to his first wife.

Marlene gave Barry more aggravation than he had experienced in hundreds of snooker promotion negotiations, and it took him over seventy telephone calls to Australia – and several increases in the purse offer – before he finally clinched the 'impossible' fight. Working closely with Dennis Roach and David Shapland of the PRO international management agency, he booked Tottenham's ground at White Hart

Lane for the fight that everybody said could not be made. Roach and Shapland, a former deputy editor of the *Sun*, were best known in the world of football. They, along with Hearn, had the advantage of not knowing anything about the politics of boxing. Mickey Duff was brought in on the promotion, and suddenly the impossible started to look possible.

Melody, Joe's first wife, was paid her alimony, but still almost sank the fight by giving a series of newspaper interviews in which she alleged that Bugner had knocked her about. Joe dismissed it as lies, and said that this was the sort of aggravation he could do without. He threatened not to come back to London, but the lure of the purse and the prospect of at last getting into the ring with Bruno persuaded him to get on the plane to Heathrow. From the moment he landed, Joe's mouth worked overtime. He spilled even more words than Muhammad Ali at his peak, and the wall-to-wall publicity made it just about the most talked-about fight in British boxing history. You could hardly turn on a television chat show, listen to the radio or open a newspaper without finding either Joe and/or Marlene in full flow. The more the Bugners talked the more Bruno liked it because he was on a percentage of the takings. Joe grumbled that he was doing all the banging of the drum, but it suited Bruno.

The strange thing about Joe and me was that despite the way we had been linked for so many years we had never really met. I had no idea what he was like behind the loud-mouthed braggat that he presented for the publicity machine. His corny scripts at times seemed to have come from those rubbishy spaghetti westerns in which he had featured during his various retirements from the ring. Some of the stupid things he said made me wonder about his sanity, but I was assured by people who knew him well that it was all an act, and that underneath the blarney he was a likeable big softy with a good sense of fun. Leading up to the fight I did not want to know about the 'nice guy' side of Joe. He had got me wound up with many of his insults, and I fed on this as my motivation to give him a good hiding.

When I at last came face to face with Bugner at the pre-fight press conference I could hardly believe the size of the man. He looked huge, and I wondered if he was exercising his body as much as his tongue.

Joe was certainly bigger than in his three impressive comeback victories Down Under where he had outpointed James 'Quick' Tillis, David Bey and the man I found so elusive, Greg Page. He said that he wanted the extra weight so that he would be able to push me around.

Joe followed his usual silly script at the conference, saying things like, 'Frank is stepping out of his class. He's strictly 'C' class while I'm A-plus. He is going to get a real bashing.' He added: 'The tension is going to get to him. He'll be a bag of nerves when the first bell goes, and long before the twelve rounds are over, only one man is going to finish on his feet. The other won't be–and I know who that will be...'

It was the perfect feed line and I dived in and said: 'You!'

There was a lot of tension between Joe and me, and it was not manufactured for the press. He was trying to do an Ali-style psyching job on me, and I was not going to stand for it. I broke the tension when somebody asked if we would have to fight bare-footed if the heavy rain that was around continued.

'I don't think the man who supplies my Nike boxing boots will be very pleased with that idea,' I said.

As it turned out the Saturday evening weather was kind to us. There was an autumn chill in the air, but both Joe and I were well wrapped up going to the ring. I was all in red, while 'Aussie Joe' wore a fancy dressing-gown in the gold and green colours of Australia. As I stared across the ring at him clutching the flag of his adopted country in his right glove during the playing of the national anthems I felt as if I was looking at one of the Australian Alps. At the weigh-in I was amazed to find Joe stepping on the scales at a massive eighteen stone four pounds, the heaviest of his career. I weighed in at a trim sixteen stone four pounds, deliberately light so that I could put into practice jab-and-move tactics.

It was one of the most satisfying performances of my career. Joe came out swinging, trying to land a quick knock-out. He had obviously believed all that rubbish about me having a weak chin, but his punches were of the flappy sort, not nuclear blows like Bonecrusher and Witherspoon had thrown. It had worked for him ten years earlier when he had bombed out Richard Dunn in the first round, but he found me a much tougher and more elusive opponent. I pulled him up in his tracks with a couple of left hooks and then started to dominate the fight with a stiff left jab that kept snapping back his head.

From the second round I concentrated on switching my attack, first banging away with both fists to the huge expanse of Bugner's belly and then going to long range to launch jabs and hooks through his high guard to his face. Joe was always trying to wrestle me to the ropes, using his enormous bulk to push me back. But I kept pulling away, claiming the centre of the ring from where I was able to pick my punches, mixing my attacks from head to body and then back to the head.

I could sense Joe tiring as I stepped up the pressure in the middle rounds. You know before anybody else when you have your opponent on the slide. You hear it in his grunts as you land to the body, and you see it in his eyes that are suddenly dulled and anxious. The sparkle had gone out of Joe, and every time I ripped punches into his ribs he sucked in deep mouthfuls of air like a winded bull. I knew it was only a question of time before I put him out of his misery.

We were into the last minute of the eighth round when I shook Joe with a right cross to the temple. He wobbled like a giant jelly, reeled across the ring and then fell slowly backwards into the ropes. There was some criticism later that I had been allowed to hit him while he was down, but the bottom rope was holding him up and referee John Coyle did nothing to stop me as I unleashed a volley of about eight punches before brave old Joe went down for a count of eight.

As he got up looking like a man in a trance I went gunning for him, but this time Mr Coyle pulled me off just as the white towel came fluttering in from Bugner's corner. The bell went at the same time, but it was too late to save poor old Joe.

I had at last laid the ghost of Joe Bugner. There were the inevitable cynics who claimed that I could not have beaten him in his prime, but I could do no more than I had done. Joe, announcing his retirement yet again, was sporting enough to say: 'Frank did a good job on me. He punches much harder and boxes much better than I thought. I gave out out a lot of bull-shit before the fight to sell tickets, but Frank has earned my full respect. He will give Mike Tyson a lot of trouble.' So old Joe wasn't such a bad guy after all. One of Tyson's managers, Jim Jacobs, was at the ringside and my win set the wheels in motion for another championship challenge.

FIGHT No. 35
Opponent: Mike Tyson (USA)
Venue: The Hilton, Las Vegas
Date: 25 February 1989
LOST by stoppage, fifth round

F RANK'S reward for beating Joe Bugner was to be named number one contender for the world heavyweight title held by Mike Tyson. We have covered the bewildering build-up to the contest in the *Tyson Revisited* chapter. There was an electric atmosphere in the indoor boxing hall at the Las Vegas Hilton, much of it generated by 2,000 British supporters. They managed to drown out the Tyson fans in the capacity 9,000 crowd with their 'Bru-no, Bru-no' chants. Frank was so deep in concentration after having had a final hypnosis session in the dressing-room that he hardly gave any attention to the preliminaries. He did not take his eyes off Tyson, and locked his gaze on him almost as if he was trying to hypnotise him as they received their final instructions.

I just wanted him to know that I was not in fear of him, and that he would not be able to intimidate me. Tyson was prowling around the ring like a caged tiger as the ring announcements were being made, and he was aware that my eyes were following him as he went through his weird routine of wriggling that massively wide neck of his as if it were an extra limb. He was dressed as usual in black shorts and wore ankle-high black boots without socks. His idea was to look like a ferocious old-style ring warrior, and it was all part of his act to try to put the fear of God into his opponents. I had made such a close study of Tyson that knew his act better than anybody, and I refused to be frightened of him. He had come in ten pounds lighter than me at fifteen stone eight pounds, his best fighting weight, which convinced me that I should forget all the stories I had heard about him not having trained properly. Both of us meant business as the first bell rang.

Tyson gave a little skip as he came out of his corner almost at running speed. I knew he would be looking to try to land an early bomb, and I was determined to get in first. As soon as we clashed in the centre of the ring I forced his head down with my left glove and fired a right that whizzed just off target. He was throwing left and right hooks with bad intentions, but I was stepping inside them. I was biting hard on my gumshield as I braced myself to withstand the sort of punches with which he had knocked Michael Spinks cold. Then suddenly one of his over-arm rights had thumped against the side of my head. My legs went from under me as if somebody had pulled the carpet away, and as I went down on one knee Tyson clobbered me with another right. The gutter tactics that I had expected from him.

I was more embarrassed than hurt. We had been fighting for less than twenty seconds. 'Please God,' I said in silent prayer, 'don't let me go out in the first.' I jumped up quickly at three because I did not want him to think he had hurt me. As referee Richard Steele counted the mandatory eight seconds I nodded in the direction of my corner to let them know that I was okay.

Tyson came roaring in at me for what he was convinced would be the kill, but I held him tight so that he could not get any leverage for his punches. He had his head down in front of me thumping away to my body, and I brought my right down on to the back of his neck. The ref, who had ignored Tyson's punch while I was on the canvas, shouted: 'Watch the rabbit punching, Bruno.'

When I immediately started holding and hitting again, the referee signalled to the judges that he was docking me a point. It did not bother me because I knew I had knocked Tyson out of his stride and that I had weathered the early storm. Tyson was still throwing plenty of leather and at a speed that was unbelievable, and I knew already that seeing him in slow-motion while under hypnosis had done nothing to help me. I was managing to block many of his blows on my arms and elbows, and I had the satisfaction of seeing a look of surprise on Tyson's face as I stood my ground and traded punches.

He had to back off as I got behind my left jab, and then he jumped in at me with a big left hook. I stepped inside it and landed with a short right followed by as good a left hook as I have ever thrown. It crashed against the side of Tyson's jaw and his legs buckled under him as if he'd been coshed. He was really body-popping, and I have since been asked a thousand times why I did not follow up with one more punch that could have put him away. I did not willingly let him off the hook. He fell against me and I could not get my arms out to get in a punch to the head. By the time the referee had pulled us apart Tyson had cleared his head, and – though I did not know it then – my chance of making history by becoming the first British winner of the heavyweight title this century had gone.

Tyson knew that he was in a fight for his life, and he started the rough-house stuff in a bid to stamp his authority on the bout. Just before the bell to end the round he caught me in the face with his elbow, and as I blinked I was aware that blood was running down from my nose. There was a roar from my army of supporters as the bell rang. I had got through the first round, which was more than sixteen of Tyson's opponents could say. He gave me a long hard stare at the end of the round, which I took as a mark of respect.

I caught Tyson with a good left hook to the body early in the second round, but he made me pay for it with a left-right combination to the head that made my ears ring. He was bobbing and weaving and I found him a difficult target to pin with any really wicked punches. I tried to claim the centre of the ring and to keep him on the end of my left jab, but he was brilliant at ducking under it and then firing uppercuts and hooks from close range. I attempted to get home with a similar left hook to the one that had caused him so much distress in the first round, but I was a whisker off target and as my punch whizzed past his jaw he fired in three rapid rights to the head that brought me up in my tracks. Watch it, Frankie. Get yourself on red alert.

In the third round I got my left hand snaking through to his head, but he came charging in at me like a bull and thumped a left hook into my face. As I held on to him in a clinch the referee again had a go at me, disregarding the fact that Tyson's head was thumping into me like a third glove. As we broke, he crashed a right over the top of my defence and I had to immediately fall back into another clinch while I waited for the spring to return to my legs. It was not the power of Tyson's punches that were causing me so much trouble as the speed of them. In those days he had the fastest hands in the business.

I was so busy trying to block his attacks that I could not raise a nuclear attack of my own. I knew I was hurting him when I was getting home with my punches because I could see his eyes glazing and his mouth dropping open, but I was not landing as often as I needed to if I was going to stop his bull-charging tactics. Just before the end of the third Tyson winced as I sank a left hook into his ribs. Moments after the bell rang he threw an angry right which gave me the satisfaction of knowing that I had got him rattled. At least I knew I was proving that I was not the push-over so many people had predicted.

I made a shaky start to round four. He hammered me with a big swinging right that made me see stars, and I was forced to hold on again. I am convinced if I had used these holding tactics against Witherspoon I would have been able to withstand his eleventh round attack. But that's history... which is what I was trying to make against Tyson. I got my jab working in the middle of the round and was just beginning to think that I was getting on top when, after at last getting a warning for butting, he unleashed a volley of lefts and rights to the head and body that knocked the wind out of me. As the bell ended the round I have to admit that I was not feeling in control of myself.

My cornermen had to work overtime during the interval, one massaging my legs, another getting water down my neck and back and Terry Lawless holding an ice-pack to my bruised and puffy face. 'You've got to keep that left jab working,' said Terry. 'And when you're in close try to throw a right uppercut. You're doing yourself really proud, but you must get that left into his face. Make him eat it.'

These were the last instructions I was to receive. The fifth was a nightmare. Tyson came swarming over me, determined to carry on where he had left off at the end of the fourth. I clung on for dear life, and the ref shouted: 'Stop holding Bruno. This is your last warning.' I wanted to say, wouldn't you hold if you were in my boots! A right and a left drove me back to the ropes, and I could feel the strength draining out of me as Tyson launched a two-fisted attack. I was doing my best to defend myself as hooks and crosses rained in from the fastest fists in history, but he unhinged me with a right hook followed immediately by a right uppercut that nearly lifted my head off my shoulders. I was still conscious but badly dazed when the referee, Richard Steele, pulled Tyson off and grabbed me before passing me over to Terry, who had been running around the ring apron preparing to throw in the towel. I'd had the granny knocked out of me, but not before letting Tyson know that I could dish out some tasty punishment of my own. 'One day,' I thought, 'I would like another crack at you Mr. Tyson.'

171

FIGHT No. 36
Opponent: John Emmen (Netherlands)
Venue: Royal Albert Hall, London
Date: 20 November 1991
WON by knock out, first round

IT was thirty-three months before Frank returned to the ring after his defeat by Tyson. In between he had become self-managed, with Mickey Duff as his promoter, and had overcome an eye injury scare that threatened to wreck his comeback plans. A routine eye check revealed that he had torn a retina in his right eye. It was mistakenly reported that he had a detached retina, which would have signalled the end. But Professor David McLeod, a genius of an eye surgeon, repaired the tear and, following a series of inspections by neutral eye specialists, Frank was given permission by the British Boxing Board of Control to resume his career. Waiting in the opposite corner for him was John Emmen, the Dutch and Benelux champion who had lost two of eighteen professional contests. He did not belong in the same arena, let alone the same ring as Bruno.

I had no idea how I would react to my long lay-off and just five rounds of boxing in the previous four years. And I was none the wiser after a fight that quickly developed into a farce and lasted exactly three minutes. From the moment I landed my first serious right hand punch in the opening minute Emmen ran away from me like a frightened rabbit. I kept hunting him with my left jab as he circled backwards around the ring, and every time I brought my right hand over he looked as worried as a man facing a firing squad.

A left to the body had Emmen sucking in his breath, and then a long right to the side of the head knocked him to the canvas. He got up straight away and clung on to me with a vice-like grip. I shook him off and hammered in a sequence of lefts and rights that sent him tumbling back to the floor. I was so anxious to finish it that one of my punches landed as he went down. Emmen was complaining about a twisted knee as he got up, but referee Mickey Vann waved us to fight on and I ended a miserable fight with a sweeping left hook.

172

FIGHT No. 37
Opponent: Jose Ribalta (USA)
Venue: Wembley Arena, London
Date: 22 April 1992
WON by knock out, second round

T HERE had been savage after-fight criticism of the choice of John
Emmen as Frank's first comeback test, and promoter Mickey Duff
knew he had to come up with a recognised world-class opponent to
silence the Bruno baiters. Nobody could accuse him of selecting a
pushover for Frank's second fight after his long lay-off. Jose Ribalta,
an American-based Cuban, had mixed in the very best company and
had lost narrowly on points to Bruno's old foes Tim Witherspoon and
Bonecrusher Smith. He had also given Mike Tyson all the trouble he
could handle before being stopped in the tenth round. The boxing
writers unanimously agreed in their big fight previews that Ribalta
had the chin and the staying power to give Bruno a real test.

Ribalta got me really steamed up before the fight by boasting to
the press that he would be throwing the sort of powerful punches
that could blind me. It was not a cheap publicity gimmick to sell tickets.
He really meant it. After all the problems I had been having with my
eye it was just about the nastiest, gutter-level thing he could have
said, and it made me determined to give him a good hiding. I did not
allow him a chance to get into the fight. From the opening seconds I
had him backing off under pressure from a stream of left jabs that
pounded through his defence. I tried a left hook, right cross
combination and I could see the sudden doubt and anxiety in Ribalta's
eyes as the punches landed. He went into his shell and I had to do all
the chasing.

It was the same story at the start of the second round, and as he
retreated to the ropes I put all my power into a looping right – my
banana bomb – that thumped against the side of his jaw. I knew it was
all over from the moment that the punch landed, He was out on his
feet, but got tangled up in the ropes as I threw another combination.
Ribalta toppled sideways to the canvas where he was counted out.
Now I really felt as if I was back.

173

FIGHT No. 38
Opponent: Pierre Coetzer (South Africa)
Venue: Wembley Arena, London
Date: 17 October 1992
WON by stoppage, eighth round

SOUTH African iron man Pierre Coetzer had given Riddick Bowe a hard time before arriving in London to tackle Bruno in an official eliminator for the IBF version of the world heavyweight title. The major problem for Frank was ring rust after only three competitive rounds of boxing in more than three-and-a-half years. Coetzer meantime had been getting a lot of rounds under his belt as he battled his way into the world rankings. Trainer George Francis tried to compensate by pushing Frank through scores of sparring rounds in the gymnasium, but there is no substitute for the real thing.

My lack of action showed in the early rounds against Coetzer, who had the toughest chin of any fighter I have ever met. It was a real Desperate Dan of a jaw. I deliberately came in at my heaviest ever weight of seventeen stone six pounds because I knew I would need every ounce of my strength to wear down the South African. I went into the ring knowing that it was one of the most important fights of my life. A victory would virtually clinch a third world title fight for me, but a defeat would have meant I had nowhere to go with my career. I was too anxious to get the job done, and in the first three rounds my timing was off and I was missing the target with too many punches. Coetzer was awkward and dangerous, like a wounded bull, and I resorted to tough tactics of my own when he started bashing me with his head. The referee gave me a couple of warnings for hitting and holding, but I just got on with trying to punch Coetzer our of my path. It was not a vicar's tea party in there. From the fourth round on I was connecting with the sort of punches that would have flattened most fighters, but Coetzer kept shrugging them off. Then, in the eighth round, a left uppercut and two rights sent him crashing through the ropes. He bravely pulled himself up, and I was unloading my big bombs when his corner wisely threw in the towel.

FIGHT No. 39
Opponent: Carl Williams (USA)
Venue: National Exhibition Centre, Birmingham
Date: 24 April 1993
WON by stoppage, tenth round

CARL Williams was nicknamed 'The Truth' because when he was an up and coming prospect somebody commented on his potential and he replied, 'Ain't that the truth'. Some of the self belief had been knocked out of 'The Truth' by the time he climbed into the ring against Frank Bruno at Birmingham's National Exhibition Centre, but he knew that a victory over the British hero could elevate him back into the world ratings. Frank knew he was one step away from a world title challenge against Lennox Lewis, and dare not slip up.

Once again, I had everything to lose and nothing to gain. If I beat Williams, they were going to say he was past his best. If I lost, I would have to wave goodbye to the fight that I wanted above all others, against Lennox Lewis. I had great respect for Williams. He was recognised as one of the best boxers in the heavyweight division, a good mover with a nice line in jabs and a right hand that could take you out if you got careless. It meant I had to be on red alert, fighting in a positive way but not taking any unnecessary risks. I went into the fight built for speed rather than strength, weighing in nearly a stone lighter than my seventeen stone six pounds against Coetzer. I knew the fight would be fought at long range, with both of us concentrating on left jabs to pave the way for rights. I was handicapped by the first serious cut of my career, with blood leaking from above my left eye from the third round. I boxed well within myself, but managed to stay in command for most of the fight. Williams had tried to match me jab for jab, but too many of his punches fell short. Going into the tenth round I decided I would try out my nuclear right because I could sense Williams tiring. He ducked low as he threw a jab. It gave me the opening for a long, chopping right to the side of his head. Suddenly he was body-popping on the canvas. He pulled himself up but as he fell back into the ropes with the count at nine, referee Davis Parris signalled that it was all over.

FIGHT No. 40
Opponent: Lennox Lewis (Great Britain/Canada)
Venue: Cardiff Arms Park
Date: 1 October 1993
LOST by stoppage, seventh round

THE WBC world title fight against Lennox Lewis has been covered in greater detail in Chapter 4, but for the record, the champion Lewis weighed in at sixteen stone five pounds – nine pounds lighter than the challenger. The fight was staged at Cardiff Arms Park, starting at 1a.m. so that it could be screened 'live' on television in the United States. Frank had never got himself in better condition.

It amused me after the fight when Lewis explained away his poor show in the early rounds to being cold. What did he expect at one o'clock in the morning in Cardiff in October? Jamaican warmth? He could not bring himself to accept that he was not so much cold as I was too hot for him. I continually beat him to the punch, and despite his reach advantage it was my jab that dictated the first half of the fight. I had him in serious trouble with my right hand in the third round, and all his smiling to the corner did not fool me. I knew I had him worried. He was moaning and groaning to referee Mickey Vann about what he claimed was my rabbit punching. That was a sign to me that I was getting the better of him. No fighter squeals to the ref if you are in command and feeling confident.

As we went into the seventh round and the second half of the fight I was well in front on most scorecards, and I was convinced that the belt was going to become my property. I had a swelling over my left eye that was affecting my vision, but it is no excuse for what happened in that seventh round. I was driving Lewis back as I had for much of the fight when a left hook knocked me dead. The last minute of the fight from then on is a blur and I only know exactly what happened from studying video replays. The referee was right to stop it while I was shifting punishment on the ropes. I have never been so disappointed. Everybody said that Lewis was the best around but, even if I say it myself, I gave him a hell of a fight and an even bigger fright. He beat me fair and square in the end, but we both knew that I had been on top.

FIGHT No. 41
Opponent: Jesse Ferguson (USA)
Venue: National Exhibition Centre, Birmingham
Date: 16 March 1994
WON by stoppage, first round

JESSE Ferguson was beaten in two rounds by Riddick Bowe in a WBA title fight ten months before he fought Frank. He had performed with credit against Mike Tyson, Bonecrusher Smith, Oliver McCall and Tony Tubbs. Only Tyson, Bowe and Bruce Seldon had managed to stop him in his thirty-one fights that had been spread over eleven years. Just thirteen months earlier he had beaten Ray Mercer. But despite his impressive pedigree he gave a performance against Bruno that did not even rise to the description of mediocre in a 'fight' that lasted precisely 142 seconds. After the referee rescued the outgunned Ferguson as he sagged against the ropes, BBC viewers were witnesses to the unlikely spectacle of Frank having a dispute on air with his great pal Harry Carpenter.

It was not my fault that Ferguson collapsed from the first attack I mounted. He had gone the distance with some of the best punchers in the business, but he just couldn't take it when I caught him with three successive rights to the head. They were solid whacks, and one that landed on the side of his ear brought a pained expression to his face. I was not that surprised to see him go down, and when he got up at a count of five I went for him with both fists. Referee John Coyle warned me for hitting on the back of the head. Then I was back in at Ferguson, who sank to the canvas after taking another four good punches. He was up at seven this time, and I moved in to finish him off and was firing away when the referee decided that Ferguson had taken enough. I was delighted with my performance considering it was my first fight since the Lewis defeat, and I was shocked when my old mate Harry started knocking the quality of the opposition in our usual ring interview. We had a bit of a barney, but I later realised he was only doing his job. But I was still happy with my win because I knew my punches had lost none of their power.

FIGHT No. 42
Opponent: Rodolfo Marin (Puerto Rico)
Venue: Shepton Mallet, Somerset
Date: 18 February 1995
WON by stoppage, first round

FRANK WARREN had taken over as Bruno's promoter, and for his first outing under the Warren banner he travelled to the unlikely boxing outpost of Shepton Mallet in Somerset. ITV were covering the fight live from the West of England Showgrounds, and imported for the occasion was Rodolfo Marin who just three months earlier had taken world-rated Joe Hipp to a ten rounds split decision. He had won twenty of his twenty-three contests and the pre-fight predictions were that he was capable of taking Bruno at least several rounds.

I was in great shape for the fight because I had been training for the fight against Ray Mercer in Hong Kong that never took place, and then for this unofficial world title eliminator against Marin. He had a reputation for being able to take a good shot, and I deliberately came in at my heaviest ever at just under seventeen stone nine pounds to make sure I had full power in my punches. I noticed that Marin seemed unusually nervous as he stood in his corner waiting for the first bell to ring, and I made up my mind to try to get to him early. I got my distance with three scouting left jabs and then threw one of my long clubbing rights that clouted Marin on the top of the head. There was a look of surprise on his face as he felt the power, and he sat down with a bump. He grabbed hold of the ropes and pulled himself up, but he was quickly back down again as I caught him with a left hook that dropped him even though it landed on his glove. Referee John Coyle reached seven with the count before spreading his arms because it was obvious that Marin had lost interest in taking any further part in the fight. There were some boos from the crowd because there had been only sixty-five seconds of action, but most of the fans appreciated what I had achieved against an opponent who, according to his ring record, had a strong chin. I took the microphone and thanked the spectators for making me feel welcome down in scrumpy land.

FIGHT No. 43
Opponent: Mike Evans (USA)
Venue: Kelvin Hall, Glasgow
Date: 12 May 1995
WON by knock out, second round

THERE was enormous pressure on Frank when he climbed into the ring at the Kelvin Hall in Glasgow to fight 'Mighty' Mike Evans. He knew that a world title contest with Oliver McCall had been arranged by the Don King-Frank Warren promotion team, and he dared not slip up against an opponent who had gone the distance with outstanding fighters like Tony Tucker, Tony Tubbs and Michael Moorer. Bruno had never had a bigger target for his punches. Evans weighed in at a colossal nineteen stone four-and-a-half pounds, and Frank also made a big impact on his return to the Sky television screens by scaling his heaviest ever seventeen stone ten pounds.

Glaswegian fans have a good knowledge of boxing, and I was keen to impress them on my debut in Scotland. They soon found out why Evans is known as 'Mighty' Mike. He was enormous, but the tyre around his middle was a sure sign that he was not the fittest man I had ever met. I was too close to that title dream of mine to allow Evans to spoil it all, and I was determined to get rid of him as quickly as possible. He could move surprisingly fast for such a big man, and retreated around the ring throughout the first round while I chased after him looking for the chance to land my softening-up jabs. Evans caught me with a surprise left-right combination just before the bell and I staggered because I was off balance. His cornermen thought he had hurt me and yelled, 'You've got him, Mike. The son of a bitch is wobbling.' But it was Evans who was wobbling like a giant jelly when I caught up with him in the second round. He kept grabbing me in a bid to stop me throwing my big bombs, but I got my range and had him down on one knee with a right to the head. When he got up at six I drove him back to the ropes and flattened him with a sweeping left hook. I had removed the only obstacle between me and a fourth crack at the world championship. Next stop Oliver McCall.

FIGHT No. 44
Opponent: Oliver McCall (USA)
Venue: Wembley Stadium, London
Date: 2 September 1995
WON on points, twelve rounds

AT last, the top of the mountain after a climb that had taken thirteen years and a lot of blood, sweat and the occasional tears. We covered the build-up to the world championship challenge against Oliver McCall in Part One. This is Frank's action replay memory of the fight of his life:

I was focused on only one thing during the preliminaries, and that was sticking my left jab into McCall's face. My game plan was to keep McCall on the end of my left lead while looking for any opportunity to crack over the right. I also knew I had to be careful not to get tagged by his crafty right that had spelled the end for Lennox Lewis at nearby Wembley Arena nearly a year earlier. I was so anxious to get to McCall that I was halfway across the ring even before the first bell rang. Referee Tony Perez, taking charge of his ninetieth world title fight, had to restrain me until the bell rang. McCall had come into the ring crying, and that was the way I wanted him to leave. I was determined to get in with the first punch, and I knocked McCall's head back with a straight left thrown from my shoulder. This was going to be Oliver's diet. I was going to fill his face with leather, just as I used to when he was my sparring partner. He was just getting used to my left jab banging through his guard when I let go with my favourite nuclear right. It rocked McCall on his heels, and he was close to going down for the first time in his career. Oliver had been smiling when the lefts were landing, but the right wiped the smile off his face and brought up a mound of a bruise beneath his left eye.

You know when you're the guv'nor. It doesn't need the points of the judges or the referee to tell you. You can see it in the eyes of your opponent, and you can feel it with every punch that lands. I knew from as early as this first round that this was going to be my night. My fight. My title. At the end of the round Oliver was not looking like a champion. He had taken a lot of punches from me in our sparring sessions together, but now he knew that they were not the real thing. He had felt the real thing during these first three minutes. And I could see in his eyes that he did not like it. There was lot more where those punches came from.

George Francis was delighted with the way I had started. 'Just right, Frank,' he said. 'Keep the jab in his face, and pick your moment for the right. Make sure you hold your left high to block his right. Start mixing some uppercuts with the straight punches.'

McCall made my life easier by continually coming to me, which made a nice change for me because I usually had to chase after my opponents. I had a good lead going into the fourth, and Oliver was being bullied by his corner into stepping on the gas. He had his first success of the fight with a couple of rights, one of which landed on my mouth and split my bottom lip. I grabbed him in the style perfected by so many American heavyweights, and the referee had to force us apart. I got a rollocking from George at the end of the round for not making more of the left jab.

I tried to get the fight back to arm's length exchanges in the fifth, but McCall was ducking inside my lead and then working so hard at close quarters that I could hear him breathing in my ear. It sounded like a steam engine. Referee Perez warned me for rabbit punching, but I thought McCall asked for it because of the way he was lowering his head as he bulled his way forward.

McCall must have thought the fight was beginning to swing his way in the sixth round until I knocked his head back with a right uppercut that came from my toes. The roar of the crowd proved that it had been a real winner, and I could make out the voice of Nigel Benn at ringside yelling: 'That's the one, Frank. The uppercut!'

We were now at the halfway point of the fight, and I knew I had built a commanding lead. But Oliver had paced himself well and I could sense an increase in his output. It was part planned by him, but also a sign of his desperation because he could feel the title slipping away from him. I had hit him so many times with my left jab that I decided by the eighth round to give him a taste of a right jab for a change. I switched to southpaw for the first time in my career. It caught McCall unawares and I kept him off balance with a right lead. He was confused, and just as he started to unload a right handed attack I switched back to orthodox.

George told me to try the switch tactics again in the ninth round, and I landed as many right jabs as lefts. Oliver was concentrating more and more on trying to take me out with his mighty right, but he was telegraphing the punch and I was able to avoid most of his bombs. He made my ears ring with a right swing halfway through the ninth but I countered with a left hook to the ribs that made him gasp.

By the tenth round I was beginning to pay for the early hot pace that I had set, and I began to almost wrestle McCall at close quarters as we lay on each other taking breathers. Because I was tired, I started getting caught by the sort of wild punches that I was easily avoiding in the first half of the fight. Again it was a right uppercut that stopped the 'Atomic Bull' in his tracks just as he started to find the range with that sneaky right. McCall must have known I was tiring because of the way I kept clutching him in the clinches, but he had taken a lot of punishment and was finding it difficult to get rhythm and power into his punches.

My worst moment of the fight so far came midway through the eleventh. I was looking for McCall's right as he backed me up to the ropes, and he thumped me with two left uppercuts that snapped my head back. I had to cling on for dear life to stop him repeating the punishment. As I returned to my corner on legs that suddenly weighed a ton, my brother Michael yelled: 'Three minutes from the title, champ. That's all. Three minutes.' George knows me better than anybody, and he realised I was close to exhaustion. 'Just go out there and grab him,' he said, knowing that this was no time for the sweet science. 'Lay on him and don't give him room for his punches. He knows he has got to knock you out to win, and he will be coming out throwing everything. Smother him and don't let him settle. It's all yours, Frank. The title is there for you.'

The last three minutes seemed more like three hours. I had to use all my willpower to stay on my feet. I had put so much into the first half that I was now feeling like a zombie. But I followed George's instructions, and laid on, held and wrestled to stop McCall taking me out with one of his bombs. It was not exactly Marquess of Queensberry stuff, but I managed to stop Oliver from landing with any combinations. He staggered me with a couple of rights, but I refused to let him follow up. I knew by the reaction of everybody at the final bell that I must have got it. Nigel Benn tried to lift me, but I was so tired that I was a dead weight. It was only when I heard the words 'and the *new* world champion' that I allowed myself to believe that my dream had at last come true.

FIGHT No. 45
Opponent: Mike Tyson (USA)
Venue: Las Vegas, USA
Date: 16 March 1996
LOST by stoppage, third round

This WBC heavyweight championship contest gets full coverage in Chapter 10. For the record, Frank weighted in at seventeen stone nine pounds, giving him a weight advantage of two stone all but a pound. He stood four inches taller than the 5ft 11in Tyson, and his 82 inch reach was longer by eleven inches. Bruno had been champion for 196 days, and this was his fifth world championship contest. Tyson was having his third contest since his three-year prison sentence on a rape charge. Before being sent to prison in 1992 he had won 41 of 42 fights, and had been the winner of eleven world title fights.

I felt completely focused on the fight, and throughout the national anthem and most of the preliminaries I kept repeating over and over again, 'I will not, I cannot be beaten.' My brother, Michael, was at my shoulder continually repeating, 'This is your time...your time.' Unfortunately, when the bell rang all my good intentions disappeared because Mike Tyson refused to concede an inch to me. He hurt me several times in the first round with explosive combination punches, and I was forced to hold on while I cleared my head. Just before the bell to end a dodgy first round I sustained a bad cut over my left eye. Round two was not much better, and referee Mills Lane took a point away from me for holding. In my opinion Tyson deserved the same treatment for dangerous use of the head and elbow. I at least managed to get in a few telling blows of my own. The third round was about thirty seconds old when Tyson launched a ferocious attack that drove me back to the ropes. He unleashed something like a dozen punches, all but two on the target. I sank down on the bottom rope, and referee Mills Lane called it all off after fifty seconds of the third round. I did not even have the consolation of really staggering Tyson, as in our first fight in 1989. I managed to catch him with some solid punches, but nothing that stopped his charges. No excuses. The better man won.

Appendix 1
The Frank Bruno Fact File

Personal: Born Hammersmith General Hospital, 16 November 1961. Christened Franklin Roy Bruno. First family home at Battersea, then at 39 Barmouth Road, Wandsworth. Weight at birth: nine pounds. Star sign: Scorpio. Mother: Lynette, a former district nurse and a Pentecostal lay-preacher. Father: Robert, a bakery worker, died in 1975.

Robert and Lynette arrived in London from Jamaica in the 1950s and set up home in South West London. Lynette was born in Jamaica, Robert in Dominica. Brothers: Michael and Eddie. Sisters: Faye, Angela and Joanne. Frank is the youngest.

Married Laura Mooney at Hornchurch, Essex, on 5 February, 1990, after being together for ten years.

The Brunos live in Essex, with their daughters Nicola and Rachel, and son Franklin.

Schools: Swaffield Primary, Wandsworth, and Oak Hall, Sussex.

Represented: Sussex schools at football and athletics. Head boy in his final year at Oak Hall. Left school in 1977. Various briefly held jobs including metal polisher, building site labourer, beer cellar worker and sports shop assistant at Lonsdales.

Started boxing at the age of nine with the Wandsworth Boys Club. Won an NABC title on a walk-over. Boxed three times as a junior. All his contests were against Gary Hill. Each bout went the distance, with Bruno winning two and Hill one.

Boxing, amateur career: 21 contests, 20 victories (avenged his only defeat by Irish international Joe Christle). Boxed for the Sir Philip Game Amateur Boxing Club, 1977–80. In his final season as an amateur he represented Young England and, at 18, he was the youngest ever ABA heavyweight champion.

Professional from 1982, following an operation in Bogota to correct short-sightedness in his right eye.

Management: He was managed for his first 35 fights by Terry Lawless, but is now self-managed, with his wife, Laura, supervising his commitments away from boxing.

Promoters: National Promotions (Mickey Duff, Jarvis Astaire and Terry Lawless). Since December 1994: Frank Warren.

Ring record 45 contests, 40 victories. His only defeats have been by James 'Bonecrusher' Smith and in world title fights against Tim Witherspoon, Mike Tyson (twice) and Lennox Lewis.

Total rounds as a professional: 170. Has won 38 of his fights inside the distance, 17 by clean knock out. European champion 1985–1986 (relinquished the title).

World WBC championship won by outpointing Oliver McCall at Wembley Stadium on 3 September 1995. Lost it to Mike Tyson in three rounds at Las Vegas on March 16 1996.

Tale of the tape: Height: 6ft 3in; weight (in pro debut):15st 7.5lbs (217.5lbs); weight (when winning title): 17st 9lbs (247lbs); reach: 82in; boots: 12in; calf: 16in; thigh: 24in; biceps: 17in; neck: 18in; chest: 47in (51in expanded); fist: 14in; forearm: 14in; wrist: 9in; waist: 34in; ankle: 10in.

Boxing trainer: George Francis. Previous trainer: Jimmy Tibbs.

Masseur: Rupert Doaries.

Outside the ring: Awarded the MBE in the 1990 New Year's Honours List.

Hobbies: swimming, training (!), driving, eating, shopping for good clothes, listening to jazz-funk and soul records, watching old boxing videos (his favourite boxers Joe Louis and Muhammad Ali).

Previous books: *Know What I Mean?* (1987), *Eye of the Tiger* (1992). **Video:** *FRANKly BRUNO* (1993).

Member of Equity, and has starred in pantomime with Michael Barrymore at the Dominion Theatre (with record box office sales), and took the leading role in panto at Nottingham in 1990–91 (again with record box office takings). In 1992–93 he played the title role in *Robin Hood* in Bristol, with Little and Large as his co-stars. Again, record box office receipts. He has made guest appearances on dozens of TV shows with among others Cannon and Ball, Lenny Henry, Freddie Starr and Terry Wogan. He was the regular presenter of the weekly BBCTV series *People*. Voted the Stars Organisation for Spastics Sports Personality of the Year for 1989 and 1990.

Runner-up to Jonathan Edwards in the BBCTV Sports Personality of the Year Award for 1995. Was voted overall 'Champion of 1995' in the inaugural Sky Sports Awards.

Awarded Variety Club Silver Hearts in 1987 and 1995 for children's charities work.

More than sixteen million viewers tuned into his *This Is Your Life* tribute from Michael Aspel in 1994.

Frank has been the focal personality in nationwide advertising campaigns for HP Sauce and Kleenex tissues.

Appendix 2
The Frank Bruno Fight File

17.03.82	Lupe Guerra (Mexico)	w.ko.1	Royal Albert Hall
30.03.82	Harvey Steichen (USA)	w.rsf.2	Wembley Arena
20.04.82	Tom Stevenson (USA)	w.ko.1	Royal Albert Hall
04.05.82	Ron Gibbs (USA)	w.rsf.4	Wembley Arena
01.06.82	Tony Moore (GB)	w.rsf.2	Royal Albert Hall
14.09.82	George Scott (GB)	w.rsf.1	Wembley Arena
23.10.82	Ali Lukusa (Zaire)	w.ko.2	West Berlin
09.11.82	Rudi Gauwe (Belgium)	w.ko.2	Royal Albert Hall
23.11.82	George Butzbach (Ger)	w.ret.1	Wembley Arena
07.12.82	Gilberto Acuna (Puerto Rico)	w.rsf.1	Royal Albert Hall
18.01.83	Stewart Lithgo (GB)	w.ret.4	Royal Albert Hall
08.02.83	Peter Mulendwa (Uganda)	w.ko.3	Royal Albert Hall
01.03.83	Winston Allen (GB)	w.rsf.2	Royal Albert Hall
05.04.83	Eddie Neilson (GB)	w.rsf.3	Royal Albert Hall
03.05.83	Scott LeDoux (USA)	w.rsf.3	Wembley Arena
31.05.83	Barry Funches (USA)	w.rsf.5	Royal Albert Hall
09.07.83	Mike Jameson (USA)	w.ko.2	Chicago
27.09.83	Bill Sharkey (USA)	w.ko.1	Wembley Arena
11.10.83	Floyd Cummings (USA)	w.rsf.7	Royal Albert Hall
06.12.83	Walter Santemore (USA)	w.ko.4	Royal Albert Hall
13.03.84	Juan Figueroa (Argentina)	w.ko.1	Wembley Arena
13.05.84	'Bonecrusher' Smith (USA)	l.ko.10	Wembley Arena
25.09.84	Ken Lakusta (Canada)	w.ko.2	Wembley Arena

(Commonwealth championship eliminator)

06.11.84	Jeff Jordan (USA)	w.rsf.3	Albert Hall
27.11.84	Phil Brown (USA)	w.pts.10	Wembley Arena
26.03.85	Lucien Rodriguez (France)	w.rsf.1	Wembley Arena
01.10.85	Anders Eklund (Sweden)	w.ko.4	Wembley Arena

(European heavyweight championship)

| 04.12.85 | Larry Frazier (USA) | w.ko.2 | Albert Hall |
| 04.03.86 | Gerrie Coetzee (South Africa) | w.ko.1 | Wembley Arena |

(WBA world heavyweight championship, final eliminator)

| 19.07.86 | Tim Witherspoon (USA) | l.rsf.11 | Wembley Stadium |

(WBA heavyweight championship challenge)

24.03.87	James Tillis (USA)	w.rsf.5	Wembley Arena
27.06.87	Chuck Gardner (USA)	w.ko.1	Cannes
30.08.87	Reggie Gross (USA)	w.rsf.8	Marbella
24.10.87	Joe Bugner (Aus)	w.rsf.8	Tottenham
25.02.89	Mike Tyson (USA)	l.rsf.5	Las Vegas

(WBC heavyweight championship challenge)

20.11.91	John Emmen (Hol)	w.ko.1	Royal Albert Hall
22.04.92	Jose Ribalta (Cuba)	w.ko.2	Wembley Arena
17.10.92	Pierre Coetzer (SA)	w.rsf.8	Wembley Arena
24.04.93	Carl Williams (USA))	w.rsf.10	Birmingham
01.10.93	Lennox Lewis (GB/Canada)	l.rsf.7	Cardiff

(WBC heavyweight championship challenge)

16.03.94	Jesse Ferguson (USA)	w.rsf.1	Birmingham
18.02.95	Rodolfo Marin (Puerto Rico)	w.rsf.1	Shepton Mallet
13.05.95	Mike Evans (USA)	w.ko.2	Glasgow
03.09.95	Oliver McCall (USA)	w.pts.12	Wembley Stadium

(WBC heavyweight championship)

| 16.03.96 | Mike Tyson | l.rsf.3 | Las Vegas |

(WBC heavyweight championship)

Appendix 3
What the Papers Said

IT was the leader writers who took over from the boxing reporters to have their say when Frank Bruno won the world heavyweight championship by outpointing Oliver McCall at Wembley on 2 September 1995 (co-inciding with the thirtieth birthday of Lennox Lewis). This is a cross section of what the papers said following Frank's victory, words that capture the special place that Frank has won in the hearts and minds of the British public...

THE SUN

What a great fight! Frank Bruno set a few people back on their heels on Saturday night. And not just shell-shocked opponent Oliver McCall. The genial giant silenced the critics who claimed he wouldn't last 12 rounds. He showed with his crisp left jab and stinging upper cut that he can really box. But most of all, Frank proved he is world class. Hail to the Champion. The *Sun* has given its own knighthood to The Great Man. John Major wants gongs for the good guys. So, how about making it official, Your Majesty?

DAILY MAIL

'I did it for myself, my family and for Britain.' So said Frank Bruno when he claimed the world heavyweight title. What excellent reasons for doing anything worthwhile. Bruno, a three time loser, made it on his fourth attempt at the title, after going the full 12 rounds against the holder, Oliver McCall. What a performer. What determination. What a dogged sense of destiny. And what a pleasure to record his success. For Bruno had many hurdles to overcome. Not only is he from a deprived working-class background. He is, as he so proudly says,

British. And in recent years the British have become more accustomed to being good losers rather than gracious winners. Worse yet, Bruno is so obviously a nice guy. And as the cynics constantly tell us: 'Nice guys don't win.' How pleasing that King Bruno has proved the cynics wrong.

DAILY TELEGRAPH

Frank Bruno was made an MBE for failing to win a world title, so heaven knows what he will get for finally capturing one. Presumably a hereditary peerage, the freedom of his home county of Essex and a portrait in the National Gallery to show that nothing is valued so highly in Britain as perseverance. For a man who exemplifies the supposedly Anglo-Saxon virtues of hard labour and persistence, Bruno has attracted more than his share of enmity since he knocked over his first opponent in March 1982. Even those who derided him for being as stiff as a fighting ironing board will have to acknowledge the audacity and bravery of this feat. Say it until you believe it: Frank Bruno, heavyweight champion of the world.

DAILY MIRROR

Frank Bruno hopes he'll become a role model to youngsters. You don't have to hope, Frank. You already are. Expelled from school and branded a difficult child, you were transformed by your own hard work and determination. When you found fame and fortune as a boxer, you never became aloof and snobbish. As Frank the pantomime dame, you are always ready to have a laugh. You left the blood lust and insults to other boxers. And when critics were writing you off as boxing history, you still had the courage to believe in yourself. Congratulations on winning the world heavyweight crown, Frank. You're a champ in more ways than one.

DAILY EXPRESS

Few sporting achievements can have touched the nation's heart as profoundly as Frank Bruno winning the world heavyweight championship. His is a victory for courage and self-belief. His delightful

191

daughter Rachel probably best summed up all our feelings about his win when, with the simplicity of the young, she said yesterday: 'It was nice.' Indeed it was. Nice one, Frank.

BOXING NEWS

The time-honoured tradition of Britain's horizontal heavyweights was buried when Frank Bruno became a world champion at the fourth time of asking. Bruno had to withstand a desperate last round rally to unanimously outpoint Lennox Lewis conqueror Oliver McCall over 12 rounds before approximately 30,000 loyal and passionate spectators on a chilly evening in the same ring where his first challenge (against Tim Witherspoon for the WBA title) failed nine years ago. It has taken Bruno 13 years to reach the top but was well worth the wait for the 33-year-old Londoner, who could no longer restrain his emotion in a tearjerking interview with Sky television's Ian Darke at ringside. Who says nice guys never win? Bruno, for so long considered the good loser, was rewarded for years of unremitting perseverance, dedication and self-belief, traits which, at long last, compensated for his lack of natural talent and weakness against big punchers. This was a triumphant occasion for British boxing, shoving aside the dark clouds which have loomed more than once in recent years and opening up a bright blue sky. The future for the first British-born heavyweight to win the world heavyweight title in the ring since Bob Fitzsimmons 98 years ago is unlimited in financial terms.

And this is a selection of what the papers had to say after Frank's defeat in his first defence of the world championship against Mike Tyson . . .

DAILY MIRROR

It would have been wonderful if Frank Bruno had won but no one can take anything away from his achievement. He is a great ambassador for sport and for his country. He is unfailingly honest and cheerful. And he has a remarkable humility for any leading boxer – particularly a heavyweight boxer. He did the nation proud and we are entitled to be proud of him. He didn't win because, as he said himself, Mike Tyson was better. But there is nothing to be ashamed of in that. Now it is time for Frank to hang up his gloves. There is nothing more that he can achieve. There will never by anyone quite like him. Frank Bruno is a one-off. An inspiration and an example to young people everywhere. A 24 -carat national treasure.

DAILY STAR

Only a very brave man would have stepped into the ring with Mike Tyson. Frank Bruno deserves a medal just for that. But it was wishful thinking to believe he could have beaten the man of iron. It's a miracle he hasn't suffered permanent injury from the bludgeoning he received in the ring at Las Vegas. Now is the time for Frank to hang up his gloves. For good.

THE INDEPENDENT

One of the things that has to be said about Bruno is that he has never lacked heart and determination. Another is that he withstands heavy head punches better than has been argued. It is not that Bruno cannot take a punch but that he has no instinct for surviving the subsequent confusion. A less courageous fighter than Bruno might have considered it prudent to be counted out from the stunning hook that almost sent him over in the second round. Instead, half blinded by blood, he fought back gamely.

THE GUARDIAN

Bruno had held the title for 197 days , an achievement of which he can be justifiable proud and which will ensure him a special standing among his fellow countrymen for as long as he lives. This, they will say, was a man who got into the boxing ring with Mike Tyson not once but twice; be will be admired for the dogged courage with which, in the course of a 14-year professional career, he found ways to overcome a complete lack of innate aptitude for the game's techniques. Tyson, of course, is the most natural of fighters, elemental in his ferocity and his understanding of how to use his limited stature against bigger opponents. Yet it must be said that the Bruno of 1996 could not match the achievement of his younger self, who had lasted five rounds in 1989 and briefly but memorably hurt a man who at the time looked the most invincible fighter since Marciano.

DAILY MAIL

As Mike Tyson was pummelling Frank Bruno senseless, it is highly likely that he knew it wasn't just another British heavyweight he was rendering horizontal but a British institution. American television had sold Bruno as more British than Big Ben, and while the world heavyweight title was his principal objective, the supremely irreverent Mr Tyson will have derived additional satisfaction from dismantling a monument to the establishment. Any establishment. What he will not have realised is that by reducing Bruno to a blood-spattered ruin, he has restored him to a state of grace in his own land. America idolises winners but Britain adores a certain kind of loser. Tyson has given us back the Bruno we know and cherish, an institution we almost lost when he outpointed the out-to-lunch Oliver McCall to win his world title six months ago.

THE SUN

Frank Bruno got a terrible pasting from 'Iron' Mike Tyson. Do us all a favour, Frank, and spare us any more agony. You've been one of our greatest sportsmen and everyone admires you – whether you're in panto or fronting HP Sauce ads. So stick to that. We don't ever want to see you on the ropes again.

You are and will remain the nation's hero.